P9-DVQ-435

S P O T L I G H T

NAPA VALLEY

ELIZABETH LINHART VENEMAN

Contents

Napa Valley 5
Orientation 10
Planning Your Time 12
Tours 13
Getting There 14
Getting Around 15

Napa and Vicinity 17
Napa Wineries 19
Coombsville Wineries 21
Oak Knoll Area Wineries............ 22
Mount Veeder Wineries............. 23
Sights.............................. 24
Entertainment..................... 25
Shopping.......................... 26
Recreation 28
Accommodations 29
Food............................. 33
Information and Services............37
Getting There and Around 37

Yountville and Vicinity 38
Yountville Wineries 38
Stags Leap Wineries 41
Sights............................ 44
Shopping.......................... 44
Recreation 45
Accommodations 46
Food............................. 48
Information and Services........... 50
Getting There and Around 50

Oakville and Rutherford..... 51

Oakville Wineries 51
Rutherford Wineries 54
Chiles Valley Wineries.............. 58
Recreation 60
Accommodations 60
Food............................. 61
Information and Services............ 61
Getting There and Around 62

St. Helena and Vicinity..... 62
St. Helena Wineries 63
Spring Mountain Wineries 70
Sights............................72
Entertainment.....................74
Shopping.......................... 75
Recreation 76
Accommodations 77
Food............................. 79
Information and Services........... 83
Getting There and Around 83

Calistoga 84
Calistoga Area Wineries............. 86
Diamond Mountain Wineries 91
Sights............................ 94
Entertainment..................... 96
Shopping.......................... 97
Recreation 98
Accommodations 101
Food............................105
Information and Services...........108
Getting There and Around 108

NAPA VALLEY

© JACEK SOPOTNICKI/123RF.COM

NAPA VALLEY

Mention California wines and most people will think of the Napa Valley, usually abbreviated to simply "Napa." Mention that you're writing a travel guide to Northern California's Wine Country and almost everyone will ask about your favorite Napa wineries. There's no escaping it—the Napa Valley is regarded as the center of everything wine in California, no matter how Sonoma, Santa Barbara, or Mendocino might jump up and down for attention.

The oft-mentioned Paris tasting of 1976, which pitted the valley's wines in a blind tasting against France's best, put the Napa Valley—and California—firmly on the international wine map: Napa Valley wines won both the red and white tasting, while other California wines placed in the top five.

The Napa Valley led the premium wine revolution in the 1980s and saw the building of some of California's most ostentatious wineries in the last two decades, most recently a grandiose castle near Calistoga. This little valley is now home to more than a quarter of all the wineries in California, despite the fact that it accounts for only about 4 percent of all the wine made in the state. The statistics speak for themselves—the Napa Valley turns out some of the best wine in California.

The valley is also a marketing manager's dream. Natural beauty, colorful history, some of the biggest names in the world of wine, and $100 bottles of cabernet all serve to draw hordes of visitors—almost five million a year at last count. They in turn are entertained by top chefs, luxury pampering, and lavish winery

© ELIZABETH LINHART VENEMAN

HIGHLIGHTS

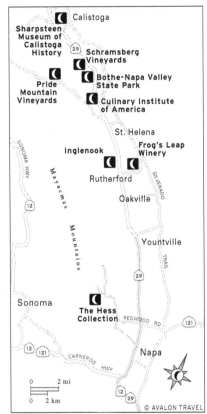

LOOK FOR ◖ TO FIND RECOMMENDED SIGHTS, ACTIVITIES, DINING, AND LODGING.

◖ **The Hess Collection:** Located in the mountains above Napa, this winery gallery brings new meaning to the expression "the art of winemaking" (page 23).

◖ **Inglenook:** This historic winery has been given a glamorous Hollywood makeover by the valley's most famous filmmaker, Francis Ford Coppola. It makes great wine, too (page 54).

◖ **Frog's Leap Winery:** Revel in the laid-back vibe at this organic winery. In addition to good wine, there's an organic garden and a free tour with tasting (page 56).

◖ **Pride Mountain Vineyards:** Straddling the Napa and Sonoma border, this mountain-top winery has some of the best views in the valley, and some of the best mountain wines (page 72).

◖ **Culinary Institute of America:** The West Coast's next star chefs are born inside this fortress-like former winery. Get a taste of their training at regular cooking demonstrations (page 74).

◖ **Bothe-Napa Valley State Park:** Take a break and stroll back in time through the redwoods (page 76).

◖ **Schramsberg Vineyards:** If you plan to visit just one champagne cellar, why not make it the most historic one in the valley? Tour the spooky cellars once visited by Robert Louis Stevenson (page 91).

◖ **Sharpsteen Museum of Calistoga History:** Learn about Calistoga's early days at this quirky little museum. It's right next to one of the original cottages from the first-ever hot springs resort in the town (page 94).

shows like no others in California, or probably anywhere else in the world.

It can all seem a bit like a giant wine theme park at times, especially when lining up at yet another ticket booth to empty your wallet for the privilege of being herded around another winery by guides who are probably as bored

as they look. It's not a great stretch to imagine that one day there will be giant gates at either end of the valley where all-inclusive passes will be sold to the "Greatest Wine Show on Earth" (the Sonoma Valley would be the parking lot if some competitive types had their way).

But though many visitors flock lemming-like

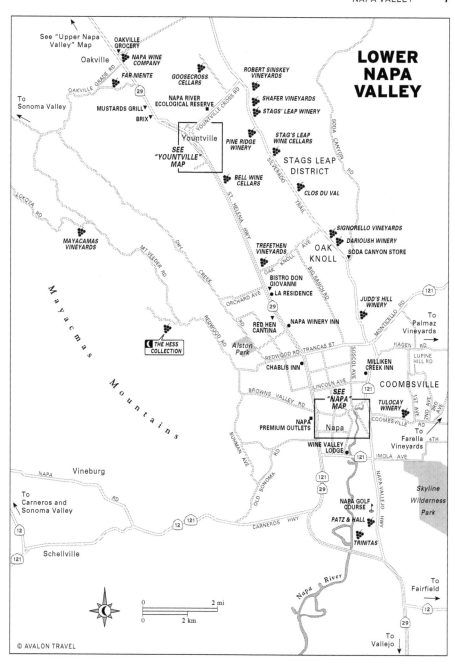

See "Upper Napa Valley" Map

LOWER NAPA VALLEY

Oakville

OAKVILLE GROCERY
NAPA WINE COMPANY
FAR NIENTE
OAKVILLE GRADE RD
GOOSECROSS CELLARS
ROBERT SINSKEY VINEYARDS

To Sonoma Valley
OAKVILLE CROSS RD
29
NAPA RIVER ECOLOGICAL RESERVE
MUSTARDS GRILL
BRIX
SHAFER VINEYARDS
STAGS' LEAP WINERY
YOUNTVILLE CROSS RD

Yountville
PINE RIDGE WINERY
STAG'S LEAP WINE CELLARS

SEE "YOUNTVILLE" MAP
BELL WINE CELLARS
STAGS LEAP DISTRICT
CLOS DU VAL

LOKOYA RD
ST. HELENA HWY
SILVERADO TRAIL
SODA CANYON RD

MAYACAMAS VINEYARDS
MT VEEDER RD
DRY CREEK
TREFETHEN VINEYARDS
OAK KNOLL AVE
OAK KNOLL
SIGNORELLO VINEYARDS
DARIOUSH WINERY
SODA CANYON STORE

OAK KNOLL
BIG RANCH RD
121
BISTRO DON GIOVANNI
LA RESIDENCE
JUDD'S HILL WINERY

M a y a c m a s
ORCHARD AVE
29
RED HEN CANTINA
NAPA WINERY INN
To Palmaz Vineyards

THE HESS COLLECTION
REDWOOD RD
Alston Park
TRANCAS ST
HAGEN RD
LUPINE HILL RD

CHABLIS INN
REDWOOD RD
MILLIKEN CREEK INN

M o u n t a i n s
BROWNS VALLEY RD
LINCOLN AVE
SOSCOL AVE
121
COOMBSVILLE
1ST AVE
2ND AVE
3RD AVE

SEE "NAPA" MAP
TULOCAY WINERY
COOMBSVILLE RD
To Farella Vineyards
4TH

NAPA PREMIUM OUTLETS
BURNHAM AVE
Napa
WINE VALLEY LODGE
121
IMOLA AVE

NAPA RD
Vineburg
OLD SONOMA RD
121
29
NAPA VALLEJO HWY
Skyline Wilderness Park

To Carneros and Sonoma Valley
12
12
121
NAPA GOLF COURSE
PATZ & HALL
CARNEROS HWY

121
Schellville
TRINITAS

To Fairfield
12

Napa River
29
To Vallejo

0   2 mi
0   2 km

© AVALON TRAVEL

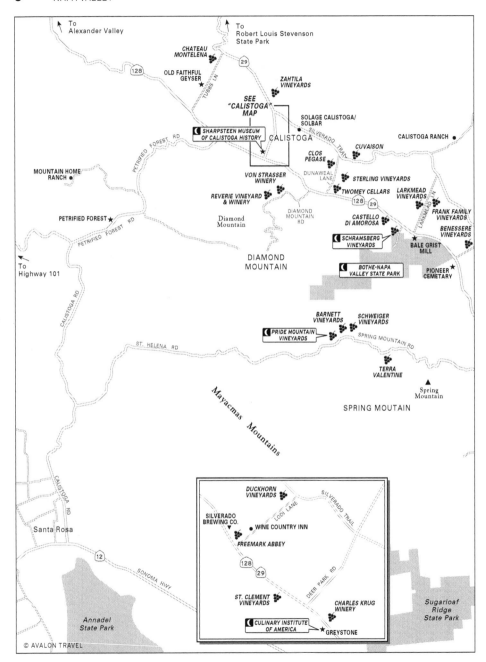

To Alexander Valley

To Robert Louis Stevenson State Park

CHATEAU MONTELENA

29

128

OLD FAITHFUL GEYSER

ZAHTILA VINEYARDS

SEE "CALISTOGA" MAP

SOLAGE CALISTOGA/ SOLBAR

SHARPSTEEN MUSEUM OF CALISTOGA HISTORY

CALISTOGA

CALISTOGA RANCH

CUVAISON

CLOS PEGASE

MOUNTAIN HOME RANCH

VON STRASSER WINERY

DUNAWEAL LANE

STERLING VINEYARDS

REVERIE VINEYARD & WINERY

TWOMEY CELLARS

LARKMEAD VINEYARDS

128 29

FRANK FAMILY VINEYARDS

PETRIFIED FOREST

DIAMOND MOUNTAIN RD

Diamond Mountain

CASTELLO DI AMOROSA

BENESSERE VINEYARDS

SCHRAMSBERG VINEYARDS

BALE GRIST MILL

To Highway 101

DIAMOND MOUNTAIN

BOTHE-NAPA VALLEY STATE PARK

PIONEER CEMETERY

ST. HELENA RD

BARNETT VINEYARDS

SCHWEIGER VINEYARDS

PRIDE MOUNTAIN VINEYARDS

SPRING MOUNTAIN RD

TERRA VALENTINE

Spring Mountain

Mayacmas Mountains

SPRING MOUTAIN

DUCKHORN VINEYARDS

LODI LANE

SILVERADO TRAIL

SILVERADO BREWING CO.

WINE COUNTRY INN

FREEMARK ABBEY

Santa Rosa

128 29

DEER PARK RD

ST. CLEMENT VINEYARDS

CHARLES KRUG WINERY

Sugarloaf Ridge State Park

CULINARY INSTITUTE OF AMERICA

GREYSTONE

Annadel State Park

SONOMA HWY

12

© AVALON TRAVEL

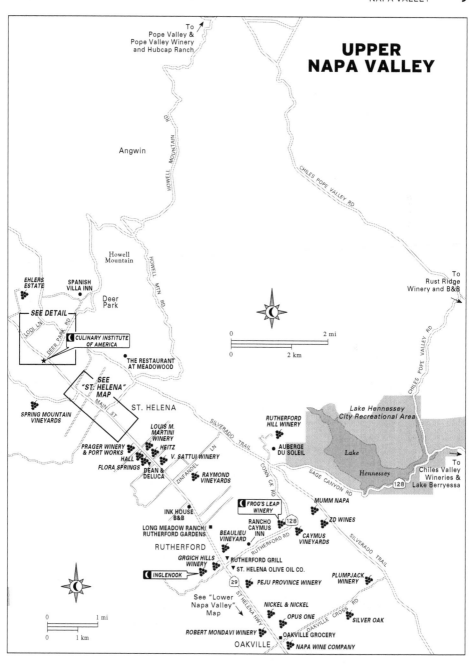

UPPER NAPA VALLEY

To Pope Valley &
Pope Valley Winery
and Hubcap Ranch

Angwin

Howell Mountain

Deer Park

EHLERS ESTATE

SPANISH VILLA INN

SEE DETAIL

LODI LN

DEER PARK RD

HOWELL MTN. RD

HOWELL MOUNTAIN RD

CHILES POPE VALLEY RD

To Rust Ridge Winery and B&B

CULINARY INSTITUTE OF AMERICA

THE RESTAURANT AT MEADOWOOD

0   2 mi
0   2 km

SEE "ST. HELENA" MAP

SPRING MOUNTAIN VINEYARDS

MAIN ST

ST. HELENA

SILVERADO TRAIL

RUTHERFORD HILL WINERY

Lake Hennessey
City Recreational Area

LOUIS M. MARTINI WINERY

HEITZ

PRAGER WINERY & PORT WORKS

HALL

FLORA SPRINGS

V. SATTUI WINERY

DEAN & DELUCA

ZINFANDEL LN

RAYMOND VINEYARDS

AUBERGE DU SOLEIL

Lake Hennessey

CONN CK RD

SAGE CANYON RD

128

To Chiles Valley Wineries & Lake Berryessa

CHILES POPE VALLEY RD

INK HOUSE B&B

FROG'S LEAP WINERY

MUMM NAPA

LONG MEADOW RANCH/ RUTHERFORD GARDENS

RANCHO CAYMUS INN

128

ZD WINES

BEAULIEU VINEYARD

RUTHERFORD

CAYMUS VINEYARDS

SILVERADO TRAIL

RUTHERFORD RD

GRGICH HILLS WINERY

RUTHERFORD GRILL

ST. HELENA OLIVE OIL CO.

INGLENOOK

29

PEJU PROVINCE WINERY

PLUMPJACK WINERY

See "Lower Napa Valley" Map

ST. HELENA HWY

NICKEL & NICKEL

OPUS ONE

OAKVILLE CROSS RD

SILVER OAK

ROBERT MONDAVI WINERY

OAKVILLE GROCERY

NAPA WINE COMPANY

OAKVILLE

0   1 mi
0   1 km

to the same big wineries, there are hundreds of others to choose from in the valley, big and small, glamorous and rustic. Such diversity is one of Napa Valley's big draws and the reason so many people keep coming back for more.

Art lovers could easily spend an entire vacation visiting the many wineries with art or sculpture displays. Photosensitive souls can hunt down all the wineries with cool, dark underground caves. Architecture buffs will have a field day at some of the more outlandish facilities, with design influences in the valley ranging from medieval to avant-garde.

And all that's before even considering wine itself. The valley is home to boutique wineries making just a few hundred cases of wine a year, and to corporate behemoths turning out millions. The multitude of microclimates has given rise to a patchwork of 16 (and counting) distinct appellations, or AVAs, where just about every major type of grape can be grown. Although this is a red wine-lover's paradise, there's a wine made here for almost every palate.

The valley's diversity extends well beyond wine: At one end of the valley are the hot springs and spas of Calistoga, while Napa at the other end contains some big-city entertainment. In between, nature offers plenty of diversions from wine, and restaurants turn out delicacies that would put many in world's finest-dining capitals to shame.

The locals are remarkably sanguine about the endless stream of visitors clogging their valley. Clearly, they are wise enough not to discourage the hands that ultimately feed them. But they also get to experience the beauty and diversity of the valley, the quality of the food, and the strong sense of community when the rest of us have long since gone home.

And, of course, they get to toast their good fortune with some of the best wines in the world.

ORIENTATION

The Napa Valley, including Carneros, is roughly 35 miles long, with two main roads running up each side of the valley and about half a dozen roads traversing the 2-4 miles between them. As far as the world's major winemaking regions go, this is baby-sized, so don't be intimidated.

Just north of Carneros is the city of **Napa** itself, the biggest settlement in the valley, home to many of the workers who keep the wine industry humming. The city was called Nappa City when it was laid out in grand style by Nathan Coombs in 1848 on a bend in the Napa River. The river connected the city to San Francisco and was pivotal to its rapid growth over the subsequent decades. It has also been pivotal to the city's ongoing modern revival since Napa embarked on the huge $300 million flood defense program after disastrous floods wiped out downtown businesses in the 1980s and 1990s and even as recently as December 2005.

It's not the most attractive city and has traditionally been bypassed by tourists speeding to the big-name wineries and trendy towns farther north, but Napa has been making more of an effort to cash in on its Victorian history, riverside setting, and namesake valley.

There are decades of neglect and terrible architecture to counter, however, and the downtown revitalization is definitely a work in progress, not helped by the 2009 recession that resulted in a new crop of empty storefronts, shuttered restaurants, and the bankruptcy of Napa's cultural shrine to wine and food, COPIA (the American Center for Wine, Food, and the Arts).

Napa also still lacks the compactness and style of other Wine Country destination towns like Sonoma, Healdsburg, or even St. Helena farther north. That is changing, however, as the city completes its massive flood-defense program, and luxury hotels and condo developments sprout along the newly secured riverbanks. The Westin hotel chain opened a luxury hotel on the riverbank in 2009, bringing with it a Michelin-starred restaurant. In 2012 the Andaz hotel, a member of the Hyatt family, added additional polish to the district. Across the river, COPIA may have gone belly-up, but in its wake the Oxbow Market has revitalized

NAPA'S SILLY-MONEY WINES

At the Napa Valley Wine Auction in 2008, six bottles of 1992 Screaming Eagle sold for $500,000. They were magnums, but that still works out to more than $40,000 per bottle or about $7,000 per glass. Granted, the auction is a charity event and therefore encourages big spending for a good cause, but there are probably no other wines that would be bid so high, whatever the occasion.

Make that *few* other wines. There were 10 magnums of Harlan Estate wine that sold for $340,000, and an eight-magnum vertical of Bryant Family Vineyards wine that sold for $290,000. Then there was the record breaker: One magnum of Alexander Valley Vineyards' Cyrus sold for a jaw-dropping $215,000 in 2013. That is $107,500 for one bottle of wine, an Alexander Valley bottle of wine, no less. Just those four lots illustrate the power of Wine Country's so-called cult wines to open the wallets of both serious collectors and those simply with more money than they know what to do with.

The cult wine phenomenon started in the early 1990s and reached a crescendo during the dot-com boom years, when a lot of people really did have more money than they knew what to do with. They bought the beautifully made, limited-production Napa Valley cabernets, like those from Screaming Eagle and Harlan Estate, probably as much to gain the cachet of owning something so rare as to resell for a profit a few years later. As with any rare commodity, lots of bidders will push up the price.

The dot-com bubble burst, but the cult wine bubble never really did. Retailers report that sales of such silly-money wines remain as solid as their prices. There's no doubting that they are good wines, made by some of the best winemakers and sourced from some of the best vineyards. Whether they're worth hundreds of dollars or more is a question often asked—though it's ultimately irrelevant, because there are plenty of people still willing to pay and to wait years to get on the exclusive mailing lists to even get a chance to pay.

A little more troubling is that the term "cult wine" is now bandied about a little too casually. It is commonly used as a marketing tool or for bragging rights, so it's no surprise that calling even the Screaming Eagles of the world a cult wine these days is as likely to elicit a roll of the eyes as an opening of the wallet.

the area. More restaurants and tasting rooms have followed, and it is now the hip foodie center of town known, appropriately, as the Oxbow District.

From Napa, the two main valley roads begin. The St. Helena Highway—more commonly known as **Highway 29**—is the well-beaten path up the valley. It passes the town of **Yountville,** dominated by increasingly upscale shops, restaurants, and hotels, then whistles past sleepy **Rutherford** before hitting what has become almost the spiritual heart of the valley, **St. Helena.** This is the town that all others in Wine Country aspire to be: pretty, upscale, full of boutiques and restaurants, yet still a fairly down-to-earth, functional place—except on those weekends when the world comes to visit and traffic slows to a crawl.

St. Helena and the surrounding big-name wineries are the main draw in this part of the valley, and rural tranquility quickly returns as Highway 29 continues north to the narrow top of the valley, where laid-back **Calistoga** has an almost frontier-town feel—seemingly torn between maintaining its slumber and being awakened by attracting more tourists to its up-and-coming wineries and famous volcanic hot springs.

Calistoga is also where the other main valley road, the **Silverado Trail,** ends. Named for a silver mine that it once served north of Calistoga, it runs from Napa along the foot of the eastern hills and is the shortcut used to get up and down the valley by locals in the summer when the other side of the valley is clogged. Anyone in a hurry to get to a spa appointment in Calistoga or a restaurant in Napa should consider cutting across the valley to the Silverado Trail if there is heavy traffic on Highway 29.

This undulating, winding two-lane road remains almost eerily quiet at times and feels like it's in another valley altogether. It's a road along which smaller wineries turn out some of the best wines in the valley, with little of the hoopla of the big showoffs farther west. It's also a road down which serious wine lovers might prefer to travel, sampling famous cabernet sauvignons in the Stags Leap or Rutherford appellations before heading up into the hills to some hidden gems on Howell Mountain or in the rural Chiles Valley.

Napa Valley Wines

The Napa Valley probably has more microclimates and soil types along its 35-mile length than any other valley in the Wine Country. The climates and the soils drew the attention of wine-loving European settlers in the 1800s, and the seeds of the modern-day wine industry were sown.

As you drive from the city of Napa north to Calistoga in the middle of summer, the temperature can rise by up to 20 degrees. Although the northern end of the valley is significantly hotter than the southern end, throughout the length of the valley there are dozens of unique microclimates created by small hills on the valley floor as well as the canyons and slopes of the mountains that define its eastern and western sides.

In addition, geologists have identified a staggering 33 different types of soil in the valley, laid down over millions of years by volcanoes, rivers, and the earth's shifting crust. The combination of soils and microclimates create a patchwork of growing conditions that could keep winemakers happy for centuries more, and that is why there are so many distinct, recognized growing regions within the Napa Valley.

The Napa Valley north of Carneros is predominantly a red wine-growing region, thanks primarily to a warm climate that ensures the most popular red grape varieties can easily ripen and attain the sugar levels needed to make the big, powerful wines for which the valley is known. White grapes and some red varietals like pinot noir can get by in cooler climates because they generally reach their desired ripeness more easily while retaining the high acid levels desired by winemakers.

The one red grape for which Napa is most famous is cabernet sauvignon. There are roughly 45,000 acres of vineyards planted in Napa County, about three-quarters of which are planted with red grape varieties. Just over half of that red grape acreage is cabernet, which means that one varietal accounts for 40 percent of all the vineyards in Napa County (about 19,000 acres). The figure is probably closer to 50 percent of all the vineyards in the Napa Valley north of Carneros, where pinot noir and chardonnay are the more dominant varietals.

That's not to say that other wines are not important here, far from it. The Napa Valley is where some of California's most distinctive chardonnay and sauvignon blanc are produced, together with increasing amounts of syrah, sangiovese, and many other minor varietals. But cabernet always has dominated the vineyards and probably always will, with chardonnay a distant second in terms of vineyard acreage, followed closely by merlot.

Most of the big Napa Valley wineries own vineyards all over the valley. They and smaller wineries also often buy fruit from other growers outside Napa Valley, so white-wine drinkers need not despair—there will usually be plenty of whites on offer, even at wineries in the big-cab appellations like Rutherford and Stags Leap. But ultimately this is a valley dominated by cabernet and chardonnay, and those looking for more unusual types of wine will want to choose the wineries they visit carefully.

PLANNING YOUR TIME

How can visitors make sense of all these wineries and avoid all the crowds? It's a $10,000 question with about 10,000 different answers. Many visitors seem to follow a similar pattern, never making it much farther north than St. Helena and sticking to the western side of the valley. If you can avoid that pattern, you're halfway to lowering your blood pressure.

The other key to enjoying the valley rather than being frustrated by it is plenty of planning. There's so much to do and so many wineries to visit that anyone simply turning up without a plan, however vague, will end up with a headache even before drinking too much wine in the sun. Visitors can get away with no preplanning in many other parts of Wine Country, but not in such a tourist mecca as the Napa Valley.

Research the type of wine that wineries specialize in before choosing which to visit, especially if you're not a big red-wine drinker. This is, after all, **the land of endless cabernet sauvignon**, but it is also a land where plenty of stunning white wines, including champagne, are made. And if you are a big cabernet drinker, this can be the place to learn much more about the king of wines—how and why a Spring Mountain cabernet is different from a Stags Leap cabernet, for example.

Alternatively, pick a theme not related to wine for a day of touring. Wineries in Napa have necessarily become adept at distinguishing themselves from their competitors to try to attract increasingly jaded visitors, a form of Wine Country evolution. Some rely on the reputation of their wines, others on **art, caves, car collections, architecture, gardens, tours, history**—the list is almost endless and provides endless employment opportunities for marketing folks.

Another option is to **abandon the car** altogether. From Napa to Calistoga, tasting rooms have opened along the valley's Main Streets, many of which are boutique wineries too small to have their own on-site tasting rooms. Fees are low, and the atmospheres are fun and relaxed. So pick what town most appeals to you, park the car, taste, shop, spa, and dine.

Or you can head for the hills, where healthy doses of nature help make the hidden wineries in the **Coombsville, Mount Veeder, Spring Mountain,** and **Chiles Valley** appellations that much more enjoyable. Unfortunately, most mountain wineries are appointment only and require some planning to visit.

If possible, avoid the peak season that runs roughly **July-October.** It brings peak crowds, particularly on weekends, peak hotel prices, and peak daytime temperatures. **April-June** is perhaps the best time to visit, when the wet winter season is finally drying out, the temperatures mild, the creeks flowing, the hills green, and the vineyards full of vivid yellow wild mustard.

TOURS

One way to visit wineries without having to worry about traffic, drinking, or cooking an expensive wine in a sunbaked car is to take a daylong organized wine tour. Someone else does the driving, you can drink until you can no longer stand, and any precious wine purchases will get transported back to your hotel probably in better shape than you.

Another advantage is that the local tour guides are knowledgeable about the valley, the wineries, and often about wines as well, making an organized tour an option worth considering if you have no idea where to start.

There are two tour companies, each offering different experiences. The **Napa Winery Shuttle** (707/257-1950, www.wineshuttle.com, $75) specializes in personal tours of the valley from Napa to Calistoga. The shuttle has a long list of local hotels it picks up from at about 10am (though they can often pick up at any hotel not on the list). It generally hits about five or six wineries with a stop for a gourmet lunch along the way. Unfortunately, the fee doesn't include tasting, but wineries will often throw in a deal or two for being with this long-standing Napa Valley business.

Beau Wine Tours (707/938-8001 or 800/387-2328, www.beauwinetours.com) is more of a custom touring company and is often the owner of the limos seen parked at some of the bigger wineries. Rent a chauffeured car, SUV, or limousine for 3-14 people for $60-95 per hour plus tax, tip, and (depending on gas prices) a fuel surcharge, and plan your own itinerary. Note that the size of the stretch limos and vans means they sometimes cannot visit smaller wineries at all, or only by prior arrangement. Beau Wine Tours has plenty of

A CASE FOR WINTER

Does visiting the Napa Valley conjure dreams of long golden afternoons tasting cabernets, soaking in the sun at some the valley's most luxurious spas, or cycling along country lanes as the vineyards turn in the heat of an Indian Summer. The unfortunate truth is that traveling during Napa's most spectacular seasons (summer and fall) can also mean horrendous traffic, crowded tasting rooms, and astronomical hotel prices. So, why not go in winter?

In fact, winter is the best-kept secret in Wine Country. Hotel prices drop by as much as 50 percent, and restaurants, eager to lure in diners, offer inexpensive prix fixe dinners and even coupons for 10 percent off or a free appetizer or dessert. In tasting rooms, free of summer crowds, pourers have more time (and patience) to give you individual attention, even sharing with you some of their favorite vintages not on the tasting menu.

The beauty (literally) of traveling in the off-season is also the weather. Rarely does it dip below 55 degrees, and Napa is often blessed with crystal-clear days. If on the chance it does rain, there are several wineries that are the perfect place to spend a drizzly day.

- Splurge on a reserve tasting at **Beringer Vineyards** and wait out the rain inside the ornate Rhine House, filled with carved wood and beautiful stained glass.

- Warm yourself with a tawny port at the **Prager Winery & Port Works** next to the famous Web Window.

- Listen to the rain hit Italian quarried stone as you sip wine or tour the vast armory and torture chamber at the **Castello di Amorosa.**

- Wander through history-soaked caves at the Victorian **Schramsberg Vineyards,** makers of some of the finest sparkling wine in the country.

- Cozy up with a glass of muscular cabernet in an over-stuffed leather chair at **Vermeil Wines.**

knowledge of the valley, however, and can offer lots of advice. It also offers private, preplanned, daylong tours starting and finishing in either the Napa Valley or San Francisco (from $125).

Napa Valley Wine Train

The age of the steam trains that first brought the masses to the valley's Victorian spas and early wineries has long gone, but a modest reminder remains in the **Napa Valley Wine Train** (1275 McKinstry St., Napa, 707/253-2111 or 800/427-4124, www.winetrain.com, $55-189). It has been kept alive by providing what the valley does best—good food and wine. The train runs 20 miles from downtown Napa up to St. Helena and back, and reservations are essential.

The idea of being cooped up on a glorious fall day watching the vineyards and wineries through the windows of a restored Pullman rail car might not seem appealing, but it's better than it sounds. The only problem is that it

eats into your day. Think of it as taking a four-hour lunch or dinner at a gourmet, if slightly unusual, restaurant with entertainment often thrown in for free. The food is beautifully prepared, the wine first-class, and the restaurant dripping with brass and mahogany. There are no comparisons to Amtrak here.

The least expensive option serves beverages only (i.e., wine) and is more of a relaxing site-seeing experience aboard the vintage train cars. From there the indulgence and price go up. You can opt for a gourmet, three-course lunch or dinner, with the option of taking a winery tour sometime along the way. Each package includes seating in a different historic car. For example, you might lunch in the 1917 Pullman Car or take an evening tour of Grgich Hills aboard the 1952 Vista Dome Car.

GETTING THERE

There were far more ways to get to the Napa Valley a century ago, when trains and riverboats brought the visitors and goods that made the valley so successful. The car has long since become the main transportation mode, though the more adventurous can still get here on public transportation.

By Car

The Napa Valley is almost the same driving distance from three major international airports—Oakland, San Francisco, and Sacramento. Driving from the airports to the city of Napa itself will take 1-2 hours, depending on traffic; from downtown San Francisco or Oakland, it's closer to an hour of driving time.

The most direct route from Oakland and Sacramento is on **I-80** (west from Sacramento, east from Oakland). Exit at Six Flags Discovery Kingdom (Highway 37), then take Highway 29 north into Napa and beyond. From Sacramento, a slightly more direct route is to exit at Jameson Canyon Road (U.S. Highway 12), a little farther north of American Canyon. This also heads west and meets Highway 29 at the Napa airport.

From San Francisco (especially downtown), it takes about the same amount of time to drive across the Bay Bridge to I-80 and north to Napa as it does to go the prettier route through Marin. This route crosses the Golden Gate Bridge on **U.S. Highway 101** to Marin County, then east on Highway 37 before Novato, which links with Highway 121 through Carneros, past the turnoff to the Sonoma Valley, and eventually to Highway 29 just south of Napa.

The Napa Valley is also easily accessible from other parts of the Wine Country, thanks to the numerous roads that cross the Mayacamas Mountains down the western side of the valley. From the Sonoma Valley, just north of Glen Ellen, **Trinity Road** winds its way east into the mountains, becoming **Dry Creek Road** in the Mount Veeder appellation, before coming down into the Napa Valley to Oakville as the Oakville Grade. Farther north in the Sonoma Valley, just east of Santa Rosa, **Calistoga Road** heads to the hills and eventually to Calistoga, or you can turn off on St. Helena Road after about three miles to cross into the Napa Valley

down through the Spring Mountain appellation and into St. Helena.

From the Russian River Valley, just north of Santa Rosa, take **Mark West Springs Road** east, eventually turning onto Porter Creek Road, which leads down into Calistoga. And from the Alexander Valley, **Highway 128** runs south through Knights Valley to Calistoga.

Try not to be in a rush if you take these routes, because they are narrow, winding, and slow, but a lot of fun if time is not of the essence.

By Boat and Bus

The most unusual way to get to the valley without driving, short of an epic bicycle ride, is on the **Baylink Ferry** (877/643-3779, www.baylinkferry.com) from San Francisco via Vallejo. The speedy catamarans leave San Francisco's Ferry Building about every hour 6:30am-7pm during the week and three times a day (11am, 3:30pm, and 7pm) on weekends for the hourlong crossing to Vallejo, which is about 12 miles south of Napa. The one-way fare is $13 for adults, $6.50 for children 6-12, and free for those 5 and under.

From the Vallejo ferry terminal (and the El Cerrito BART station), route 10 of Napa Valley's **VINE** (707/251-6443 or 800/696-6443, www.ridethevine.com) bus service runs directly to downtown Napa about every hour until 7pm, but only during the week. It's about a 65-minute journey to Napa (except for a few times of the day when the bus makes stops) and is a bargain at $5.50. Route 10 also continues through Yountville, St. Helena, and to Calistoga; check the schedule for details on this route.

Taking the ferry and bus to the valley and then renting a bike in downtown Napa, St. Helena, or Calistoga for a couple of days would certainly make for a memorable Wine Country experience, but it might not be for the impatient or those traveling on weekends.

GETTING AROUND
By Car
Seemingly everyone drives to the Napa Valley,

so you'd think everything would be geared up for the cars transporting those five million annual visitors to this part of the world. Wrong! This is essentially agricultural land that its custodians battle to protect, so the mighty vine and strict planning laws limit a lot of development—including, evidently, road widening.

The 28-mile drive from Napa to Calistoga up **Highway 29** can take less than 45 minutes in the middle of a winter day. Try that same drive on a summer weekend or a weekday during the evening rush hour and it might take close to double that time. The sheer volume of traffic is really what slows things down, especially with so much traffic coming and going from the multitude of wineries and the traffic bottleneck of St. Helena's Main Street.

Heading north on Highway 29, you can be lulled into a false sense of security as you zip toward St. Helena, only to hit a wall of traffic about a mile south of the town caused by traffic lights that seem to meter only a dozen cars at a time onto Main Street. Heading south from St. Helena from mid-afternoon until evening on many days, your average speed is likely to be less than 20 mph until well after Rutherford. The mid-valley traffic situation is not helped by the countless turnoffs for wineries from Rutherford to St. Helena that also slow traffic. Make your life easier and use the empty center lane of the road to turn left into wineries or when turning left out of wineries to merge into traffic. That's what it's there for.

The almost constant traffic jams on Highway 29 are also a reason to discover the **Silverado Trail,** running north-south on the other side of the valley. There might be the occasional slowdown caused by a valley visitor unfamiliar with its dips and bends or who is simply lost. Usually, however, this is the domain of merciless local speed demons zipping up and down the valley at 60 mph, a feat usually possible even when the road through St. Helena across the valley is at a standstill. Many locals will use the Silverado to bypass St. Helena altogether, cutting back to Highway 29 when necessary using one of the many small cross-valley roads.

Napa is the only city in the valley to have made an effort to ease traffic flows, with its brief stretch of smooth-flowing freeway and frustrating yet effective one-way system downtown. The irony, of course, is that so many valley visitors bypass the city for destinations up-valley, so traffic is usually light anyway.

By Bike

Picking the right route at the right time of the day and exploring a section of the valley by bike can be one of the most enjoyable ways to experience the Wine Country. Whether you plan a long bike ride up the Silverado Trail or a short hop around a few Rutherford-area wineries, there are a handful of established places to rent well-maintained bicycles in Yountville, St. Helena, Calistoga, and Napa. All know the area from a biker's perspective and so will have plenty of suggestions on routes—from easy rides of a few miles to epic loops through some of the best mountain appellations. Helmets, locks, bottle cages, and puncture repair kits are always included with rentals. It's also worth asking about free roadside assistance should you get a flat, or pickup service for any winery purchases.

Touring on a bike is easy in almost every part of the valley thanks to the flat landscape (on the valley floor, at least) and the proximity of all the wineries. The only place you might want to avoid is the stretch of Highway 29 between Oakville and St. Helena, which is the scene of regular car accidents—probably caused by inattentive, lost, or simply drunk visitors. It's also such a busy stretch of road that you might not want the hassle of car-dodging anyway. However, in Yountville there is a mile-long bike path, the **Napa Valley Vine Trail** (www.vinetrail.org), which runs along Highway 29. In a town that is relatively easy to ride in, the trail may seem redundant, but the ultimate goal is to have the trail extend from Napa all the way to Calistoga.

The best stretches of valley to explore on a bike include the **Silverado Trail** in the Stags Leap District, where big-name wineries like Clos du Val, Pine Ridge, Shafer, Stag's Leap, and Robert Sinskey are all along a three-mile stretch of winding road. Just beware the speed demons on the Trail. Other easy rides include many of the cross-valley roads, which sometimes have fewer wineries per mile but also have far less traffic. Biking the Rutherford Road from Highway 29 to the Silverado Trail, for example, takes in Beaulieu, Frog's Leap, and Caymus. Then a few hundred yards down the Silverado Trail are Mumm and ZD.

The **Coombsville** area east of the city of Napa is also worth exploring on bike, not only because it has relatively quiet and flat roads but also because of its proximity to the hotels and amenities of the city. You could leave your hotel after breakfast, visit a couple of small wineries and have a relaxing picnic, then be back in Napa by mid-afternoon.

A couple of companies can do all the work and planning for your bike tour. All you need to do is show up and pedal. To plan an entire vacation centered around biking in the valley, try **Getaway Adventures** (2228 Northpoint Pkwy., Santa Rosa, 707/568-3040 or 800/499-2453, www.getawayadventures.com), which offers day, weekend, and weeklong all-inclusive packages, including hotel, meals, bike, tour guide, and shuttle van. Weekend packages are $899-1,000, and 4-6-day packages run

$1,299-1,959, with prices depending on both luxury and the number of days. Tours are usually offered once a month and take in the Napa Valley and parts of northern Sonoma. The day trips cost $149 and include the bike, helmet, water, lunch, and a guided tour of about five wineries in the Calistoga area.

Napa Valley Bike Tours (6795 Washington St., Bldg. B, Yountville, 800/707-2453, www. napavalleybiketours.com), based in Yountville, offers two daylong touring options. The most basic, the Classic Napa Valley Bike Tour, visits 3-4 wineries beginning at 9:30am and finishing around 4pm. The $139 fee does not include the tasting fees, but does include a catered gourmet picnic. If the sight of all the lovely straight rows of vines snaking up and down hills with pristine dirt between them appeals to your inner mountain biker, there's even a day trip offered that takes you biking through the vineyards of Bouchaine Winery in Carneros for $159. An additional $100 will buy you the Pedal, Pamper, and Plunge Package. This all-day excursion throws in a spa treatment and lounging by the pool at the North Block Spa in Yountville. Plain old bike rentals to go it alone cost $39-65. The company also offers free delivery and pickup of two or more bikes to hotels and B&Bs south of St. Helena.

Napa and Vicinity

Many people bypass Napa, heading up to the middle of the valley to start their wine-tasting day, but there's plenty happening this far south as well. Napa is chock-full of tasting rooms, and the city is bordered by one of the best mountain appellations in the valley as well as two of the newest AVAs. All are home to historic and modern wineries, small and large.

Just east of the city of Napa is the newest of the Napa Valley's 16 appellations, **Coombsville.** Small in terms of vineyard acreage (under 1,000 acres) and the number of wineries, it has begun to nevertheless turn out some noteworthy wines as distinct as any in the valley

thanks to a patchwork of different soils and microclimates, from sun-soaked hillsides to cool, breezy lowlands. It is an ideal place to grow both Bordeaux varietals as well as cooler-climate varietals like pinot noir and riesling. The cabernets and merlots made here have a more restrained, Old World style than those from warmer up-valley vineyards, so lovers of big, burly Napa Valley wines might be disappointed.

To the north, and stretching across the valley floor from the Silverado Trail to the St. Helena Highway is **Oak Knoll,** the other new addition to the Napa Valley's appellations. Here,

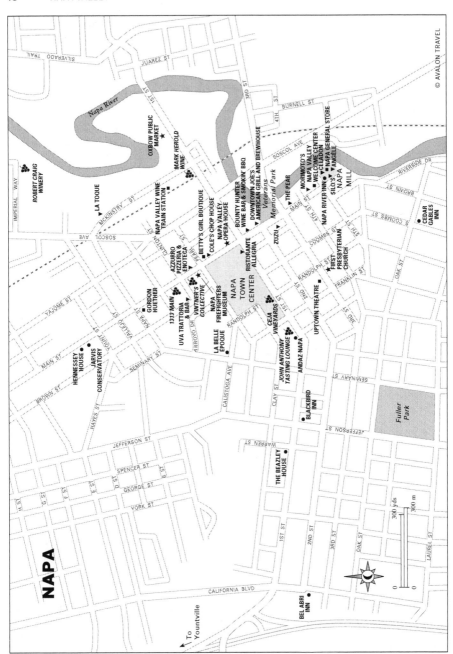

© AVALON TRAVEL

the climate is a blend of the cooler weather in Carneros, south of Napa, and the hotter mid-valley temperatures. Just about every major grape varietal is grown here, though the appellation is probably best known for whites such as chardonnay and sauvignon blanc. It is also one of the few places in the valley where varietals such as pinot noir and riesling do well.

West of the Oak Knoll appellation is the **Mount Veeder** appellation, which extends all the way from Napa up the middle of the valley on the slopes of the Mayacamas Mountains to the highest ridges and the Sonoma County line, and from as far south as Carneros and north to the Oakville Grade. Compared to the Spring Mountain and Diamond Mountain appellations farther north on the slopes of the same mountain range, Mount Veeder wines have a leaner, more mineral edge to them. The thin volcanic soils provide little nourishment for the struggling vines, and the region is far enough south to feel the cooling effects of the bay. The conditions result in elegant, age-worthy cabernets with good acidity and an earthiness lacking from mountain appellations farther north. Syrah and zinfandel are also grown on the mountain slopes and produce wines with a distinct sense of place.

NAPA WINERIES

TRINITAS

Situated in a cool cave beneath a hilltop vineyard, the **Trinitas Tasting Room** (875 Bordeaux Way, Napa, 707/251-3017, www.trinitascellars. com, 11am-7pm daily, tasting $20) functions as the resort wine bar for the Meritage Inn. The bar is open to both hotel guests and passersby, offering tastings of Trinitas wines and bites of cheese, fruit, and tiny gourmet goodies. Seats at the bar make it easy to get comfortable and stay awhile—which quickly becomes a possibility as soon as tasters get their nose inside a glass. Trinitas wines do not tend toward down-market hotel freebies. These surprisingly balanced, well-crafted wines are more than worth your time, even if (or especially if) you're serious about your vintages. Expect a small list featuring one or two whites, a rosé, and one or two

red wines, all sold at shockingly low per-bottle prices, especially compared to other Napa wines of similar quality. If you happen to be a guest at the inn, wander into the cave at about 5pm for the free daily tasting of two wines—sometimes Trinitas, sometimes guest vintners.

PATZ & HALL

The shared vision and expertise of four friends—Donald Patz, Anne Moses, Heather Patz, and James Hall—forged the creation of the **Patz & Hall** winery (851 Napa Valley Corporate Way, Ste.-A, Napa, 877/265-6700, www.patzhall.com, 10am-4pm Wed.-Sun., tasting $20) in 1988. With the assistance of some of California's best grape growers, the quartet achieved their lifelong dream of crafting benchmark, single-vineyard pinot noirs and chardonnays. Today, Patz & Hall is an acclaimed, award-winning winery producing artisan wines. Visit them at their stylish Napa Valley tasting "salon," which fuses the elements of wood, glass, granite, leather, and suede in the design, resulting in a comfortable and inviting place where wine lovers gather to indulge their passion for fine chardonnay and pinot noir. Or check out one of their monthly events at their Sonoma winery. One event includes barrel samples, a flight of four current releases paired with cheese and charcuterie from Oxbow Cheese Merchant and The Fatted Calf, and a special bottle for the group to enjoy after the tasting.

Downtown Tasting Rooms

You could spend a whole day, or even two, sampling wines from the dozen tasting rooms in the city of Napa itself—a process that's made a lot cheaper with the Taste Napa Downtown wine-tasting card, available at the **Napa Valley Welcome Center** (600 Main St., 707/251-5895, Napa, www.napavalley.org/nvcvb.html, 9am-5pm daily). The cards are also available online through the **Downtown Napa Association** (www.donapa.com), which produces the passes. However, you must allow enough lead time to make sure it reaches you by mail before you arrive in Napa. Costing $25, the card pays for tastings at twelve downtown tasting rooms. Check online for participating wineries.

Without the card, tasting prices range from a couple of dollars up to $25 at the larger collectives (though you can keep the quality Riedel tasting glass at the Vintner's Collective). Many of Napa's tasting rooms are the only places to taste the wine of some of the valley's smallest wineries, and the winemakers themselves will sometimes be pouring the wines on weekends.

VINTNER'S COLLECTIVE

The biggest tasting room is the **Vintner's Collective** in the historic stone Pfeiffer Building (1245 Main St. at Clinton St., Napa, 707/255-7150, www.vintnerscollective.com, 11am-6pm daily, tasting $25). A house of ill repute during its Victorian youth, it is now the public face of 19 different wineries and winemakers, most notably the zinfandel specialist D-Cubed, and the pinot noir specialist Ancien Wines. The regular tasting includes a flight of five wines, while the more expensive tasting adds four more-expensive wines. Parking is free, although limited.

CEJA VINEYARDS

On one side of the defunct Napa Town Center is the public outpost of Carneros-based **Ceja Vineyards** (1248 1st St., Napa, 707/226-6445, www.cejavineyards.com, 11am-6pm Sun.-Thurs., 11am-8pm Fri.-Sat., tasting $10-15). The large space is part wine-tasting bar and part art and entertainment venue, featuring a rotating display of works from local Hispanic artists. Both reflect the Mexican roots of the Ceja family, the eldest generation of which epitomized the American dream as children of immigrant farm workers who worked their way to becoming vineyard owners and finally winery owners in less than three decades. At least one member of the extended Ceja family is likely to be behind the bar to tell the story. Ceja makes only 5,000 cases of wine a year, but all the major varietals are represented from Ceja's cool-climate vineyards in Carneros and farther west near Petaluma. The Carneros Chardonnay and Pinot Noir, along with the bargain-priced

red blend Vino de Casa, are among the standouts. The white house blend has the flavor and price to be a great summer picnic wine.

JOHN ANTHONY TASTING LOUNGE

As Napa continues to evolve and reach out to the younger set, its tasting rooms have taken on a city chic. **John Anthony Tasting Lounge** (1440 1st St., Napa, 707/265-7711, www.johnanthonyvineyards.com, 10am-10pm Sun.-Wed., 10am-midnight Thurs.-Sat., tasting $20-30), next to the new Andaz hotel, looks more like a classy café than your typical tasting room. The white and black color scheme is warmed up with dark wood that seems to glow, particularly in the after hours when John Anthony really comes alive. Whether you stop in during the day, or swing by before or after dinner, you can opt for a flight of three wines ($20 or $30), a glass ($8-70—no kidding), or a bottle. For serious wine lovers, a seated tasting is available during the day by appointment and includes a cheese pairing. The winery is principally known for its cabernet sauvignon, sauvignon blanc, and syrah.

1313 MAIN

Stylish and new, **1313 Main** (1313 Main St., Napa, 707/258-1313, www.1313main.com, 4pm-10pm Tues.-Thurs., 2pm-1am Fri.-Sat., 2pm-10pm Sun.) is tasting room/wine bar/lounge/retail shop with a selection of 1,300 different wines (California as well as international) of which 13 reds and 13 whites (including sparkling and rosé), along with 13 kinds of beer, are poured nightly in two- or five-ounce tastes or sold by the glass. Like John Anthony, the interior of 1313 Main is thoroughly modern. The plush wraparound sofas, deep rust-colored chairs, textured wood, and back lighting exude a certain cool that appeals to visitors and late-night industry types. There are two bars, one of which pours only sparkling on weekend nights, and a patio lush with plants to warm its modernist edge. Feeling a little peckish while drinking late into the night? 1313 Main serves small plates of cheese, charcuterie, and spreads.

MARK HEROLD WINE

Across the river and next to the Oxbow Market, **Mark Herold Wine** (710 1st St., Napa, 707/256-3111, www.markheroldwines.com, 11am-5:30pm Thurs.-Tues., tasting $20-60) is a must-stop for both the casual drinker and the hard-core oenophile. Known up and down the valley for his cabernets, Herold's recently opened tasting room, filled with beakers, test tubes, and other science-oriented knickknacks, features not only his wines but also those wineries he consults with. The result is a heady selection of not only great, but also approachable wines. The tasting fee may seem steep, but the price gets you six tastes that include unusual Latin varietals such as grenache, tempranillo, and albariño that are made into the blends Flux and Acha. Cab lovers can indulge themselves with his hallmark wines in the pricier tasting. Either way, let your pourer know your preferences and he will be sure to accommodate you. Prices for bottles range $16-200.

COOMBSVILLE WINERIES

The rolling hills and country lanes to the east of the city of Napa are home to an increasing number of small wineries that coexist alongside horse farms, sheep pastures, and the giant Napa Valley Country Club. In a valley of big wineries and big traffic jams, exploring this area by car or on a bike is a welcome respite from the more hectic parts of the valley. Due to local planning codes, all the wineries in this area require an appointment.

FARELLA VINEYARD

Tom Farella has been a grape grower in this part of the Napa Valley for decades, so to say he knows Coombsville fruit well is perhaps an understatement. He still sells most of his estate fruit to other wineries, but he also makes about 1,200 cases of his own wines a year under the Farella and Farella-Park labels, with a more varied portfolio than many small producers. Tasting includes a sauvignon blanc, merlot, cabernet sauvignon, syrah, and the proprietary blend, Farella Alta.

The small **Farella Vineyard** (2222 N. 3rd Ave., Napa, 707/254-9489, www.farella.com, by appointment daily, tasting $20) is nestled in the trees at the end of a long driveway cutting through the vineyards, and, depending on the time of year, Tom's personalized tour might involve a walk through the vineyards or a tasting of some barrel samples.

PALMAZ VINEYARDS

With a 100,000-square-foot four-story cave system extending underground and complete with its own elevators and a computerized carousel of giant fermentation tanks, this winery could be in a James Bond movie. It's actually the home of **Palmaz Vineyards** (4029 Hagen Rd., Napa, 707/226-5587, www.palmazvineyards.com, tours and tasting by appointment only, $60) and was hailed as an architectural and engineering marvel when it was completed in 2009 after a reported eight years of construction costing $20 million. This is not just a wine aging cave like so many others in the Napa Valley; it's a huge gravity-flow winery facility built entirely underground with its own water treatment plant and the world's largest reinforced underground structure at its center. Only in the Napa Valley could you have a reproduction of a medieval castle at one end of the valley and an underground castle at the other.

Thankfully, the wines are just as impressive as the structure, and most can be tasted as part of the pricey, appointment-only tour that takes place with a family member and includes small bites of gourmet food to pair with the wines. Book well in advance because every tour is private, so only a handful of visitors can visit each week.

Most of the wine made here is cabernet sauvignon that costs upward of $120 per bottle. Typical of Coombsville cabernets, it is a more Old World style with more elegance and less sheer power than cabernets from elsewhere in the Napa Valley. A very burgundian style of chardonnay is also made here with less buttery oak and more crispness than many in Napa Valley. If you're lucky, you might also get to taste the very limited-production riesling, sourced from a cool spot in the nearby Oak Knoll District, and the wonderfully aromatic Muscat Canelli dessert wine.

TULOCAY WINERY

Bill Cadman has been making wines in this part of the world under the Tulocay label since 1975 and previously worked at some of the biggest wineries in the valley, making him one of the Napa Valley's modern pioneers and his winery the oldest in Coombsville. Yet he still manages to fly under the radar in this valley of superstar winemakers and super egos, quietly going about his business making a few hundred cases each of chardonnay, cabernet sauvignon, syrah, and pinot noir from locally grown grapes, as well as a big, bold merlot and monster zinfandel from farther afield in the Sierra Foothills. This is a refreshingly down-home winery operation.

Tulocay (1426 Coombsville Rd., Napa, 707/255-4064, www.tulocay.com, by appointment, tasting $20) is perhaps best known for its elegant, age-worthy pinot noir and both a traditional (for Napa, at least) barrel-fermented chardonnay and an unoaked, stainless steel-fermented version, along with two cabernets. Taste all with him under the oak trees at his tasting table and you'll better understand what makes this part of the Napa Valley such a unique spot for growing cabernet. You'll also likely hear plenty of local history and gossip.

OAK KNOLL AREA WINERIES
TREFETHEN VINEYARDS

One of the southernmost and oldest wineries of Napa Valley lies just a stone's throw from Highway 29 and is worth the short detour even if you're heading for the more famous wineries farther north. **Trefethen** (1160 Oak Knoll Ave., Napa, 866/895-7696, www.trefethen. com, 10am-4:30pm daily, tasting $15-25) was established in 1886 as the Eshcol winery and, unusual for the valley, is made entirely of wood.

The old Eshcol name graces the approach road to the winery and a cheaper range of wines not sold at the winery, but the building, with its large brick patio and pretty gardens (including a 100-year-old cork-oak tree), is lovingly preserved and appears on the National Register of Historic Places. The historic structure is primarily used for barrel storage and hospitality, yet it's still worth taking the appointment-only tour offered each morning at 10:30am ($25) to see the upper levels in all their musty wooden glory. Otherwise you can get a peek at the solid redwood beams and trusses in one of the barrel rooms open to the public on the ground floor, right next to the cozy tasting room.

Trefethen is perhaps best known for its chardonnay, which grows well in the slightly cooler southern end of the valley. It also makes a good dry riesling, a decent cabernet sauvignon, and a host of other wines. Tasting four of the estate wines costs $15. For an additional $10, you can taste some of the reserve wines in the wood-paneled Wine Library.

The Trefethen family was the driving force behind the decade-long quest to have Oak Knoll designated as an official AVA in the Napa Valley—the title was finally bestowed in 2004.

DARIOUSH

This Persian palace rising from the vineyard flatlands just north of Napa is one of the more unusual additions to Napa Valley's ever-colorful architectural mash-up. The winery of Persian immigrants Darioush and Shahpar Khaledi, **Darioush** (4240 Silverado Trail, Napa, 707/257-2345, www.darioush.com, 10:30am-5pm daily, tasting $18 and $40) is a hard-to-miss winery, thanks in part to the 16 giant sandstone pillars, each topped with a double-headed bull, that take the place of more traditional trees in front of the main entrance. The theme is continued in the luxurious interior, where carved sandstone looks like it's straight from the set of *Raiders of the Lost Ark,* but it still manages to blend seamlessly with designer furnishings, architectural lighting, and stainless steel trim. If you have to wait for the crowds to thin out at the glass-topped tasting bar, take a seat on what looks like (and probably is) a Le Corbusier leather sofa.

About half the winery's total production is the Signature cabernet sauvignon, a luxurious wine made with all five Bordeaux varietals. Other wines include, appropriately, a shiraz—the grape is named for the Shiraz region of Iran, where it was once believed to have originated (recent DNA analysis disproved this); coincidentally, Shiraz is also where the Khaledis grew up. Merlot, cabernet franc, and chardonnay round out the wines sourced from the winery's 75 acres of Napa Valley vineyards. Darioush also makes a small amount of pinot noir from the Russian River Valley.

Wineries by Appointment

JUDD'S HILL

This small winery at the southern end of the Silverado Trail is beginning to make a big reputation. **Judd's Hill** (2332 Silverado Trail, Napa, 707/255-2332, www.juddshill.com, 10am-4pm daily by appointment, tasting $15) is named for Judd Finkelstein, the ukulele-playing son of Art Finkelstein, who was one of the founding partners of St. Helena's Whitehall Lane Winery. After selling the Whitehall business in the late 1980s, Art established Judd's Hill, and it has since become a thoroughly family affair. His wife, Bunnie, together with Judd and his wife, Holly, all take active roles, with Art and Judd the resident winemakers.

Only 3,000 cases of wine are made here, but the complex cabernet sauvignon remains the mainstay and accounts for about half the production and many rave reviews. The flagship wine is a cabernet sourced from the hillside estate vineyards and exhibiting dusty tannins and a long finish. A few hundred cases of a rich, juicy petite sirah from Lodi-area vineyards are produced, along with a rustic Napa Valley syrah and a light, elegant pinot noir from the vineyards around the winery. Judd's Hill also makes a proprietary red blend called Magic, so named because Judd not only works his magic on wines and the ukulele but also on audiences as an amateur magician.

SIGNORELLO VINEYARDS

Visiting **Signorello Vineyards** (4500 Silverado Trail, Napa, 707/255-5990, www.signorellovineyards.com, general tastings 10am-5pm daily by appointment, tasting $25-35) is a nice reassurance that small wineries can still thrive in the big-time Napa Valley even without attaining cult status. The winery is best known for its estate cabernet sauvignon, which now dominates the winery's small production. Limited-production estate chardonnay is also made, along with the semillon and sauvignon blanc blend, Seta. Set back from the road on a hill with an idyllic view from its sunny poolside patio, Signorello is a pleasant enough stop on a daily tasting schedule. The best way to experience the winery, its wines, and the wonderful patio, however, is through the various food-related tastings offered Thursday-Sunday in the summer. Prices generally run $25-45 per person. Check the website for current food and wine activities.

MOUNT VEEDER WINERIES

◖ THE HESS COLLECTION

The art is probably going to be more memorable than the wines at this mountain estate (4111 Redwood Rd., Napa, 707/255-1144, www.hesscollection.com, 10am-5:30pm daily, tasting $10) just 15 minutes from downtown Napa. That's not to say the art of winemaking has not been perfected here. It certainly has, but the soaring four-story gallery linking the two historic stone winery buildings is the biggest draw. It houses part of the private contemporary art collection of winery founder and Swiss entrepreneur Donald Hess.

Most of the contemporary paintings and sculptures are by lesser-known European artists discovered by Hess through his artistic grapevine, though works by some big names like Francis Bacon and Frank Stella are also there. While lost in the art, it would be easy to forget this is a winery but for a couple of large windows looking from the gallery onto the inner workings of the winery itself, one framing a bottling line that could itself be called a piece of industrial art.

Complimentary tours are available at 10:30am and 3:30pm daily, or opt for the free iPod-guided tour of the gallery and the barrel room off the lobby, which is open to visitors and offers a glimpse inside of one of the original winery buildings. The tours and the $10 wine-tasting fee make Hess a great and affordable place to stop, but if you want to spend a little more, the winery offers other tasting options. A private tour and tasting is only $25, and $40 buys you a two-hour tutorial on wine and wine tasting with a certified sommelier (Sun. 1pm). For $65-85, you can pair your tasting with cheese, chocolate, or small bites. Reservations are required for both, but may be made the same day.

Wineries by Appointment
MAYACAMAS VINEYARDS

Rising up to 2,400 feet, **Mayacamas Vineyards** (1155 Lokoya Rd., Napa, 707/224-4030, www.mayacamas.com, tasting and tours 8am-4pm Mon.-Fri. by appointment, complimentary tasting) are some of the highest in the region, giving the wines a cool mountain character that few other Napa Valley wineries can match. Established in 1889, this historic stone winery now produces an earthy and concentrated cabernet sauvignon with great aging potential, as well as a crisp, oak-free chardonnay that will also mellow with a couple of years of aging. Those two wines account for the bulk of the 4,000-case production. Mayacamas also produces smaller quantities of outstanding sauvignon blanc, merlot, and (unusual for this appellation) pinot noir.

SIGHTS

In an attempt to lure St. Helena-bound visitors to the valley, Napa made a big push to recast itself as a hip and historic place that's a Wine Country destination rather than a series of exits off the freeway. The effort has been going on for nearly a decade and was not helped by the 2009 recession, which still seems to keep many storefronts vacant here even as big expensive resorts are filled to capacity farther up the valley.

Still, there are signs that the effort is paying off. One of the biggest boosts was a result of the flood abatement program that revamped the city's **River Front District** and the historic commercial area along Main Street. On top of the new floodwall sits a wide promenade and a few mixed-use developments including the overly corporate-looking **Riverfront Complex** and the charmingly revived **Napa Mill** (www.historicnapamill.com), which used to be where steamships docked before the automobile age. Both have been ushering in new upscale shops and noteworthy restaurants. The Riverbend Performance Plaza at the Napa Mill hosts free music and art shows on weekends.

The cultural anchor of the River Front District is the recently restored **Napa Valley Opera House** (1030 Main St., Napa, 707/226-7372, http://nvoh.org). La Scala it isn't, but the 1880 Italianate building is a reminder of Napa's Victorian boom times. The opera house is one of a handful of pre-1890 buildings scattered around downtown. In fact, Napa has more buildings that survived the 1906 earthquake than any other city or town in this part of the Wine Country. At one end of the spectrum is the fabulous Gothic Victorian **First Presbyterian Church** (1333 3rd St., Napa, 707/224-8693, www.fpcnapa.org) at 3rd and Randolph Streets, built in 1875, and at the other is the 1888 **Semorile Building** (975 1st St., Napa), just around the corner from the opera house and now home to the **Bounty Hunter** restaurant (975 1st St., Napa, 707/226-3976, www.bountyhunterwinebar.com, 11am-10pm Sun.-Thurs., 11am-11pm Fri.-Sat., plates and entrées $6-18).

At the north end of Main Street, the **Napa Firefighters Museum** (1201 Main St., Napa, 707/259-0609, www.napafirefightersmuseum.org, Wed.-Sat. 11am-4pm, free) makes a perfect 30-60-minute stop. The antique fire trucks and fire engines dominate the one-room museum, which is staffed by volunteers who truly love history and firefighting. But don't let the cool equipment completely overwhelm you; small artifacts and collections of vintage photos tell the story of the Napa Valley. Though there's no admission charge to come and check out all the neat stuff in this great small museum, it's nice to put a few dollars into the donation box to help keep the organization afloat.

An easy-to-follow walking tour of Napa's

Napa's River Front District

historic buildings is available from the **Napa Valley Welcome Center** (600 Main St., 707/251-5895, Napa, www.napavalley.org/nvcvb.html, 9am-5pm daily). Also available are maps for the self-guided **Art Walk.** Over a dozen modern art installations can be found in the heart of downtown, mainly along 1st and Main Streets. Hunting for Napa's sculptures is another way to see the city.

Across the river, COPIA, also known as the American Center for Wine, Food, and the Arts, was perhaps the biggest casualty of Napa's fluctuating economy. Closing its doors in late 2008, COPIA left a big hole in Napa's aspirations, which has been thankfully filled by the emergence of the **Oxbow Public Market** (610 and 644 1st St., Napa, 707/226-6529, www.oxbowpublicmarket.com, 9am-7pm daily) next door. This food-centric indoor marketplace and restaurant hub has not only drawn visitors to the other side of the river, it has ushered into being a cool new Napa neighborhood known as the **Oxbow District.** As the market continues to evolve, the surrounding streets have begun to fill up with new tasting rooms and eateries. And the empty COPIA site? There is talk of it becoming another mixed-use space with restaurants, retail shops, a high-end hotel, and high-density housing units.

ENTERTAINMENT

There's usually something going on in the bars and restaurants along bustling Main Street in downtown Napa's River Front District, especially on Wednesday nights, when the Downtown Napa Association organizes live music and nearby restaurants and shops stay open late. The schedule changes frequently, so check their website, www.donapa.com, for more information. In general, however, Napa is not a city with much active nightlife, and there are only a handful of small venues that cater to live entertainment, mainly of the jazz variety.

A popular casual jazz venue is **Uva Trattoria & Bar** (1040 Clinton St., Napa, 707/255-6646, www.uvatrattoria.com)—and it's not a bad place to eat either. There is music from the Leo Cavanaugh Trio and the big-band sound of the

Gentlemen of Jazz (6:30pm-9pm Wed.-Sat.), together with some occasional visiting artists. On weekends, Uva Trattoria keeps its doors open until midnight. Another Napa eatery with live music three nights a week is **Downtown Joe's** brewery and grill (902 Main St. at 2nd St., Napa, 707/258-2337, www.downtownjoes.com). Music is varied and ranges from rockabilly to Latin to jazz; there's a live DJ on Sunday nights. Joe's stays open until 1:30am Friday-Sunday.

At the Napa Mill complex, **Silo's** (530 Main St., Napa, 707/251-5833, www.silosnapa.com) has become as popular for evening wine tasting or a predinner drink as it has for its live music, featured almost every night. Cover charges vary (free-$25) depending on the band. Wines on the decent wine list have far lower markups than at most local restaurants, and there is also a small food menu of appetizers, pizza, and desserts.

Napa might not be the center of the valley's wine scene, but it is the cultural center. The **Napa Valley Opera House** (1030 Main St., Napa, 707/226-7372, http://nvoh.org) is home to just about every performance art *except* opera. This 130-year-old Napa institution hosts comedians, jazz ensembles, musical acts, theater performances, and even old movie nights. In fact, you can count on something going on nearly every night of the week. Countless cultural icons from Jack London to Steve Martin have walked the stage over its long history, but the building itself is also a treat.

For opera fans, the first Saturday of every month is Opera Night at Napa's **Jarvis Conservatory** (1711 Main St., Napa, 707/255-5445, www.jarvisconservatory.com), a few blocks north of the opera house, opposite the grounds of a rather bleak-looking high school. It's a casual night of entertainment provided by local Bay Area singers accompanied by the conservatory's musicians, a bit like a greatest hits of opera. The $15 ticket price includes wine and snacks during the intermission, and the entertainment usually starts at 8pm.

A bit more contemporary entertainment can be found at the renovated **Uptown Theatre**

(1350 3rd St., Napa, 877/686-5366, www.uptowntheatrenapa.com). Originally opened in 1937, this art deco theater now hosts acts from Lindsey Buckingham to Steven Wright to Boz Scaggs. Shows generally start at 8pm.

SHOPPING

The city of Napa is a slightly schizophrenic place as far as shopping goes, having to cater to its large working-class population, downtown office workers, and visitors alike. Many locals frequent the car-friendly big box stores and supermarkets that line Trancas Street north of downtown Napa. Many visitors make a beeline for the outlet mall west of downtown next to Highway 29. Food-loving locals and visitors alike frequent the Oxbow Public Market east of downtown.

For a long time, downtown Napa felt like a ghost town much of the week. But now it seems as if downtown is catching up. The River Front District has been attracting new and dynamic businesses, and the Napa Town Center shopping mall, a pastel-colored 1980s concoction generally worth avoiding, has just been bought by one of the folks behind the Oxbow Market. Hopefully, it too will be touched by the same magic and enjoy a new life as the dynamic open-air shopping and dining center it is planned to be. As of this printing, ground is expected to be broken on the project May 2013.

If you don't want to miss out on the bargains at **Napa Premium Outlets** (629 Factory Stores Dr., Napa, right off Highway 29, 707/226-9876, www.premiumoutlets.com, all stores 10am-9pm Mon.-Sat., 10am-7pm Sun.), head across the freeway on 1st Street from downtown. A typical modern outlet mall, there are 50 stores that include Ann Taylor, Michael Kors, J Crew, BCBG Max Azria, and Calvin Klein.

Looking for clothes? A quirky and more original option can be found downtown at **Betty's Girl Boutique** (1144 Main St., Napa, 707/254-7560, 11am-6pm daily except Wed. and Sun.). A vintage clothing store (mainly for women), Betty's carries used clothes that are

NAPA VALLEY FESTIVALS AND EVENTS

MARCH

Valley festivals don't get going until the **Mustard, Mud, and Music** festival in Calistoga kicks it off on the second Saturday in March. The next week is the **Taste of Yountville,** usually held on the third Saturday of March. Both are big street parties featuring local restaurants, entertainment, wineries, and stores. Count on discounted spa packages in Calistoga and a steal on Michelin-starred food in Yountville.

MAY

Anyone thinking that Napa Valley food and wine doesn't mix with rock and roll could not be more wrong, at least during the second weekend in May. The five-day, three-stage music festival **Bottle Rock** pairs 60 bands like The Shins, Flaming Lips, and Primus with 40 wineries and 28 Napa Valley eateries. Tickets are pricey: Expect to pay from $139 for a day pass to $399 for a four-day pass.

JUNE

Summer begins with big blowout sales at the **Napa Valley Wine Auction** (Napa Valley Vintners, 707/963-3388, www.napavintners. com/auctions) usually a three-day event over the first weekend in June. The annual charity event brings together the valley's biggest wine names and some very big wallets to wine, dine, and bid sometimes crazy prices for barrels and bottles of wine, all for a worthy cause. Most of the pricey tickets are sold by invitation only; the few available to the general public usually sell out early in the year.

JULY-SEPTEMBER

The most all-American event of year is the **Napa County Fair and Fireworks** (www. napacountyfair.org). On the long 4th of July weekend, Calistoga dons its best red, white, and blue (or "reds, whites, and blues") and puts on a summer festival that would make even Norman Rockwell nod in approval. A parade marches through town, fireworks explode after the sun goes down, there is a Ferris wheel, bull riding, and, of course, plenty of music, food, and wine to wash it all down.

The **Robert Mondavi Summer Music Festival** (888/769-5299, www.robertmonda-viwinery.com) in July and August has become a summer institution in the Napa Valley and features big-name rock, jazz, blues, and Latin music artists (Blondie, Ziggy Marley, k.d. lang, Dave Brubeck). The outdoor concerts are held Saturday evenings on the Robert Mondavi winery grounds, usually from the beginning of July through mid-August. Tickets cost $60-115.

The celebration of music continues in August with the month-long **Music in the Vineyards** (707/258-5559, www.napavalleymusic.com) series of chamber music concerts. The festival kicks off in early August and features a concert every couple of days at wineries and other venues up and down the valley.

Downtown Napa is host to the **Napa Town & Country Fair** in August at the Napa Valley Expo Fairgrounds (www.napavalleyexpo.com), a kid-friendly arts, crafts, and culinary celebration. The free **Napa River Wine and Crafts Fair** (707/257-0322) takes over streets in downtown Napa in early September.

NOVEMBER-DECEMBER

Flavor! Napa Valley (www.flavornapavalley. com), held on the weekend before Thanksgiving, has a higher purpose than simply indulgence—it raises money for scholarships to the Culinary Institute of America at Greystone. The festival lasts five days with events scattered up and down the valley that include wine tasting, culinary demonstrations, and discussions with some of the area's biggest names, like Thomas Keller and Masaharu Morimoto.

The valley's wine caves also have pretty good acoustics, as you can discover at one of the weekend **Carols in the Caves** (707/224-4222, www.cavemusic.net) concerts from late November through December.

in great condition and somehow retain their hip edge.

A few blocks away on 1st Street, art lovers can view the latest from local mixed-media artist **Gordon Huether** at his gallery (1465 1st St., Napa, 707/255-2133, www.gordonhuether. com, 11am-7pm Mon., Tues., and Thurs.-Sat., 11am-5pm Sun.). Huether specializes in glass and is known for his big civic installations. For art that is a little more accessible, turn east on 1st Street to the **Grand Hand Gallery** (1136 Main St., Napa, 707/253-2551, www. thegrandhand.com, 11am-6pm Mon.-Thurs., 11am-8pm Fri.-Sat., noon-5pm Sun.), which showcases American arts and crafts at its best. While the gallery has rotating exhibits, it also sells finely crafted wares like wooden bowls, unusual pottery, and unique clothes made from handspun fibers.

Just as unusual, but with a food bent befitting Wine Country is the charming antiques and gift store **Heritage Culinary Artifacts** (610 1st St., Stall 14, Napa, 707/363-4052, www.heritageartifacts.com, 9am-7pm daily), at the Oxbow Market across the river on 1st Street. Some of the culinary treasures found here from around the world are so unusual that you might be tempted despite their high price tags.

The best place to find a gift in Napa is probably the **Napa General Store** (540 Main St., Napa, 707/259-0762, www.napageneralstore. com, 8am-5pm daily) in the redbrick Napa Mill complex. Alongside the café and wine bar, the store sells a huge range of Wine Country products including cookbooks and cooking supplies, specialty foods, wine accessories, soaps from the Napa Soap Company, and even some furniture, all with some link to the Napa Valley. If you're looking for a Napa gift for anyone, this should be your first stop.

RECREATION
Skyline Wilderness Park
Most people don't associate Napa Valley with serious mountain biking, but just outside the city of Napa is **Skyline Wilderness Park** (2201 Imola Ave., Napa, 707/252-0481, www.

skylinepark.org, 8am-7pm daily), which hosted the U.S. round of the Mountain Bike World Cup three years in a row in the late 1990s. It's not the prettiest park in the valley—that distinction goes to Bothe-Napa Valley State Park near St. Helena—but it does offer 16 miles of trails for bikers, hikers, and horseback riders through its 850 acres of meadows and woodland. Spring is probably the best time to come, when the meadows are full of wildflowers doing their thing before the dry season turns the grassland to golden brown.

The park is reached from downtown Napa on Imola Avenue. The day-use fee is $5; be sure to pick up a map when you arrive because the trail system is more complex than most. Hikers should look out for bikers and horses—all users share all the trails.

Mountain bikers wanting to try their skills on the world cup route should ride from near the park's entrance for about a mile up Lake Marie Road before turning right onto the murderous ascent of Passini Road and then descending on the rocky, sometimes steep single-track of the Bayleaf Trail. The next stage of the cup was the Manzanita Trail, reached by climbing back up Lake Marie Road to the fig tree. The undulating two-mile trail was described as one of the best single-tracks on the cup circuit.

Disc golf offers some less traditional exercise. You might know it as Frisbee golf, but the Professional Disc Golf Association would prefer you use the D word instead. It is played exactly as you might think, like golf but throwing a Frisbee instead of hitting a little white ball. There is an 18-hole course, and, in case you don't always travel with one, Frisbees (sorry, discs) are available at the entrance kiosk, along with course maps. The dress rules are a little more relaxed than on most traditional golf courses—no collared shirts or fancy shoes are required. In fact, you don't even have to wear shirts or shoes.

Those who'd prefer to expend less energy can find **picnic areas** near the park entrance and about 2.5 miles up Lake Marie Road at the lake itself.

Alston Park

Untouched by either vineyards or development, **Alston Park** instead has sweeping views of both from the western fringe of the city of Napa. The park is off Dry Creek Road, reached by driving west from Highway 29 on either Redwood Road or Trower Avenue. There's no entrance fee, and the park is open dawn to dusk, although the only map is on an information board.

It's not on quite the same scale as Skyline but still offers plenty of picnicking, hiking, and biking possibilities in its 150 acres of rolling hills and meadows and along five miles of trails. There are picnic tables and a canine common where dogs can be let off the leash—a rarity in the relatively dog-unfriendly valley. Just avoid the park during the middle of hot summer days unless you're training for a desert trek, because there are few trees and little shade.

Golf

The southern end of the valley is where all the biggest and most exclusive golf courses are, many of them not open to the public. Among those that are, the biggest is the 18-hole **Napa Golf Course** (2295 Streblow Dr., Napa, 707/255-4333, www.playnapa.com, call for tee times) at Kennedy Park a couple of miles south of downtown on Soscol Avenue, which eventually becomes the Napa-Vallejo Highway. The 6,500-yard, par-72 championship course costs $21-38 to play during the week for nonresidents and $24-48 on weekends. Rates vary depending on time of day. It has a driving range, practice putting greens, and a fully stocked golf shop.

River Tours

Napa is the best place to take advantage of the river, especially during the hot dry summer. **Napa River Adventures** (1147 1st St., Napa, 707/259-1833, www.napariveradventures.com) offers tours (adults $50, children $25) that launch from the Kennedy Park Boat Dock at 2399 Streblow Drive and take a leisurely two-hour route through wetlands and alongside the historic downtown. The small covered motor launch has cushy seats and massive wraparound windows. Bring along a picnic and a bottle of wine to make the most of your pleasure-cruising experience. Or you can opt for kayak tours ($85) that last for three hours and head farther north where the river, while still smooth, feels a bit more wild and overgrown. The company also rents kayaks ($65/day, $75 for doubles), but requires reservations 48 hours in advance.

ACCOMMODATIONS

Although it feels a little removed from all the wine action in the valley, and is not the most picturesque Wine Country town, the city of Napa provides the widest choice of accommodation options. Many major chain hotels can be found here (including some recent upscale additions) as well as cheap independent motels, Victorian B&Bs, and a couple of modern boutique hotels. Best of all, rooms are generally cheaper here than anywhere else in the valley, especially at the low end of the market.

Another advantage of staying in Napa, particularly if you're not a cabernet sauvignon fan, is its proximity to the Carneros region, the land of pinot noir and chardonnay. It's just a 15-minute drive south to many wineries in the eastern half of Los Carneros, or a 15-minute drive north to some of the Napa Valley's best cabernet producers. And for those traveling to or from Oakland or San Francisco, Napa has the shortest drive time of any of the valley's towns—a full 45 minutes closer to San Francisco than Calistoga, for example.

The city is also home to a good selection of restaurants, most within a short walk of most downtown hotels and B&Bs. Indeed, if you don't want to drive to dinner but still want to choose from more than a handful of restaurants, then Napa is probably the best place to stay in the valley.

Under $150

There are more lodging options at the low end of the price spectrum in and around Napa than anywhere else in the valley. A little north of downtown Napa is the **Chablis Inn** (3360 Solano Ave., Napa, 707/257-1944 or

MORE THAN JUST HOT AIR

Hot-air balloons have become so synonymous with the Napa Valley that locals barely even blink when they float overhead in the early morning. There are still plenty of people willing to pay to get up before dawn for this unique adrenaline rush followed by a serene aerial view of the valley and its spectacular wineries.

Most companies are farther south in the valley, especially around Yountville, but a couple farther north can float the bleary-eyed over some of the volcanic scenery at the northern end of the valley. Early morning winds tend to be southerly, so pick a company that launches north of any place you really want to see from the air, but also bear in mind that balloons generally don't float far—often only a few miles over the course of a flight.

The drill is more or less the same for any ballooning adventure, whatever the company: get up before the sun rises and its rays start to generate unstable warm air that balloon pilots hate; get to a prearranged pickup point by 6am-7am (depending on the season), usually a hotel or restaurant near the launch site (some companies will also collect customers staying locally); drive to the launch site and watch, sometimes take part in, the inflation of the balloon; then finally take off with the roar of the burners for an hour-long, silent drift at elevations ranging from treetop to several thousand feet, depending on the conditions. Brunch usually follows, either at a local restaurant or alfresco in a meadow, and the whole experience usually lasts about four hours.

Some companies will do a "double hop," leaving those unfortunate enough to be assigned to the second hop, or flight, of the day following behind the balloons in a van to the landing spot before finally getting a flight. The drawback of the second flight (apart from the feeling of having woken up early for nothing) is that air currents can die down after the sun rises and the balloon might not float very far.

Ask if a double hop is planned—they tend to be more common during the busy summer and fall seasons. If it is, insist on hopping on board with the first group.

Ask how big the basket is and how many groggy souls will be crammed in with you. Some companies limit riders to 8 or even 4 people; others take up to 16 per flight. For a large premium, most also offer the option of a private flight for two.

Farthest north in the valley is **Calistoga Balloons** (888/995-7700, www.calistoga-balloons.com, $219), which launches from the Calistoga area and offers a champagne breakfast at Solage afterward for $30. Other post-flight options include a tour and tasting at Castello di Amorosa ($275) and brunch at Meadowood, followed by a tour and tasting at Bennett Lane Winery ($349). Deals are available, so check the website for special rates and discounts. **Napa Valley Aloft** (www.napa-valleyaloft.com, $220-245) has been in the Napa Valley balloon business since the 1970s and leaves from the Vintage 1870 Marketplace building in Yountville. Transportation to the launch site is available from Napa to St. Helena for an additional $15.

Balloons Above the Valley (707/253-2222 or 800/464-6824, www.balloonrides.com, $230) usually launches from near the Domaine Chandon winery in Yountville and offers a private brunch after the flight. It also sometimes has good online deals, including no-frills flights that are shorter, foodless, and cheaper. The company offers a free shuttle from anywhere in the valley. Also launching near Domaine Chandon is **Napa Valley Balloons** (707/944-0228 or 800/253-2224, www.napa-valleyballoons.com, $215). Unlike most companies, Napa Valley Balloons offers only one package, but thankfully, it is one of the least expensive in the valley. It even includes a post-ballooning lunch at Étoile at Domaine Chandon.

800/443-3490, www.chablisinn.com, $140). Some big-hotel touches (newspapers, free high-speed Internet access, HBO, CD players, and whirlpool tubs in the bathrooms) sweeten the appeal of the otherwise small and well-worn motel-style rooms. Its location right next to the St. Helena Highway (Highway 29) puts it in easy reach of wineries but also means there's some traffic noise to contend with, and you must drive to reach local restaurants in Napa and Yountville. A new mall across the street, Redwood Plaza, at least puts decent coffee within easy reach, and nothing is too unbearable considering the rates are as low as these.

Across town and a little off the beaten track is the **Napa Discovery Inn** (500 Silverado Trail, Napa, 707/253-0892, www.napadiscoveryinn. com, $150), a small and relatively clean motel with a decent list of amenities and rooms starting at $85 midweek, rising to almost $200 on summer weekends. It's in a quiet part of town but not really close to any major attractions, so you'll definitely need a car if you plan to stay here.

$150-250

For just a few dollars more a night than the nearby motels you could stay in, the more hotel-like **Napa Winery Inn** (1998 Trower Ave., Napa, 800/522-8999, www.napawineryinn. com, $190) is a sprawling building just off Highway 29 on the northern edge of Napa. The bland building is nothing much to look at, but it has nice gardens and plenty of clean and comfortable rooms that are a step up from most motel rooms. Standard amenities include Internet access, air-conditioning, and enough room for a desk. Some have refrigerators and microwaves or full kitchenettes, and three of the deluxe king rooms have whirlpool tubs.

The **Wine Valley Lodge** (200 S. Coombs St., Napa, 707/224-7911, www.winevalley-lodge.com, $170) is a simple, clean, and bargain-priced independent motel let down only by its location about a mile south of downtown Napa, putting it just out of walking distance to most good restaurants and shops. It is just off Imola Avenue, however, which provides a

quick connection to Highway 29 and wineries to the north and south. The guest rooms are simply but tastefully furnished, though with the ubiquitous motel-standard floral bedspreads made of some sort of synthetic material that feels like it could stop a bullet. Still, the Wine Valley Lodge boasts a significant past: In the late 1950s and early 1960s, several movies were filmed in Napa, and various A-list stars, including Rock Hudson, Jean Simmons, and even Elvis himself stayed at the lodge during filming. If you're a movie buff, ask for the Elvis suite!

The choice of Victorian B&Bs in Napa can be a bit bewildering. One establishment that has some of the cheaper rates and plenty of room options is **Hennessey House** (1727 Main St., Napa, 707/226-3774, www.hennesseyhouse.com), about six blocks north of downtown Napa. The only downside to the location is the particularly ugly high school across the road. Six rooms in the main Queen Anne-style Victorian house cost $159-249, depending on season, all with private bathrooms and some with four-poster beds and claw-foot tubs. Four larger, more ornate rooms, with fireplaces, whirlpool tubs, and CD players, are in the Carriage House and cost $199-329. The full gourmet breakfast is enough to soak up plenty of wine during those morning wine tastings, and the sauna is a place to relax tasting-weary feet at the end of a winter day. Allergy sufferers be warned: The resident cat has free rein of the common areas.

Anyone fed up with Victorian frills should check out the ◖ **Blackbird Inn** (1755 1st St., Napa, 707/226-2450 or 888/567-9811, www. blackbirdinnnapa.com, $185-300), an arts and crafts-style shingled house dating from the 1920s with furnishings to match the era's relatively clean and simple lines. It's just a few blocks from downtown Napa, directly opposite the West Coast home of *Wine Spectator* magazine, making it probably the most conveniently located B&B in Napa. The inn is owned by the Four Sisters group, which also owns this and a handful of other small Wine Country inns—although there's no corporate feel to the place. The only disadvantage is that there are no owners living there to take care of any late-night problems, but there are advantages, too. Unusual for a B&B, there are TVs with DVD players in every room (the walls supposedly have some decent soundproofing, unlike those at many B&Bs) and free wireless Internet access in addition to the more common fireplaces and whirlpool tubs in some rooms.

Just a couple of blocks from the Blackbird Inn and touted as Napa's first B&B when it opened in the 1980s, **The Beazley House** (1910 1st St., Napa, 707/257-1649 or 800/559-1649, www.beazleyhouse.com, $235), with its own feline resident, is in another squat shingled mansion, this one dating from 1906 and adorned with rather garish blue-and-white canopies over the windows. Rooms contain the usual mix of what look like your great-grandmother's best furnishings. The five guest rooms in the main house have private bathrooms, though only one of the five has a claw-foot tub, and cost $190-260. The other five rooms are in the Carriage House and are more luxurious, with whirlpool tubs, fireplaces, individual air-conditioning, and views of the lush garden; they cost $240-340.

Like a set for a real-life game of Clue, the sprawling mansion that is home to the **Cedar Gables Inn** (486 Coombs St., Napa, 707/224-7969 or 800/309-7969, www.cedargablesinn.com, $225) might have you wondering if you'll bump into Colonel Mustard in the study. Built in 1892 by a renowned English architect, the huge Tudor-style mansion covered in cedar shingles was one of the grandest houses in Napa County in its heyday and the site of many lavish balls and gatherings. Today the labyrinth of stairways, passages, and secret doors is home to a lavish B&B with nine guest rooms, all exquisitely furnished with Victorian finery. All have private bathrooms, four have fireplaces, and four have whirlpool tubs. Other amenities include free wireless Internet access and a gourmet breakfast befitting the surroundings. The inn has an ideal location in a peaceful residential neighborhood about a 10-minute walk to downtown Napa

and a similar distance from the restaurants at the Napa Mill.

Arguably one of the finest Victorian B&Bs in Napa is **La Belle Époque** (1386 Calistoga Ave., Napa, 707/257-2161 or 800/238-8070, www.labelleepoque.com, $250), a glorious Queen Anne-style mansion built in 1893 with an antique-stuffed interior that looks like the movie set for an Agatha Christie mystery. The six guest rooms are all unique, most with stained-glass windows, some with canopy beds, and others with fireplaces or whirlpool tubs. Standard amenities include TVs with VCRs, high-speed Internet access, and CD players, and all guests are invited to evening wine receptions featuring wines from local wineries or from the inn's own big wine cellar. All this pampering and history, plus a very central yet tranquil location, comes at a cost. Rates range from $180 for a couple of the rooms midweek in midwinter up to $300 on summer weekends. Two suites in a separate Victorian house across the street go for $309-379 more.

Despite being somewhat marooned right next to the freeway opposite the outlet stores, the **Bel Abri Inn** (837 California Blvd., off 1st St. at Hwy. 29, Napa, 877/561-6000, www.belabri.net, $189) offers good value for the money and convenience, but is not the most stylish accommodation in the city. The clean, modern building is furnished in a faux French country style and has 15 rooms, including a few with patios or fireplaces. In terms of amenities and services it lies somewhere between a motel and a hotel, but it does offer a few luxury touches like concierge service and an evening wine and cheese tasting. Downtown Napa is a little too far to walk comfortably, but it is only a few minutes' drive.

Over $250

Napa's first and still most unique boutique hotel, the **Napa River Inn** (500 Main St., Napa, 707/251-8500 or 877/251-8500, www.napariverinn.com, $250) has perhaps the best location in the city at the historic redbrick Napa Mill, a small riverside food and entertainment complex only a 10-minute walk to more shops and restaurants in downtown Napa. The 66 guest rooms are spread among three buildings—two are part of the historic mill itself and one (the Embarcadero building) was built in 1997. All rooms are furnished in an eclectic mix of contemporary and either Victorian or nautical styles, many with fireplaces, balconies, or views, though the views vary wildly from a parking lot to the river. Unlike many hotels, even the boutique variety, there is a complimentary hot breakfast brought to your room.

Giving the Napa River Inn a run for its money is the 141-room **Andaz Napa** (1450 1st St., Napa, 707/687-1234, www.andaz.hyatt.com, $250). A member of the Hyatt family, Andaz replaced the Aviva hotel in late 2012. Like its predecessor, it employs a cool urbane style to compete against the Wine Country Victoria aesthetic of most inns in Napa. Flowery bedspreads and ornate antique furniture are replaced by modern minimalist lines, crisp white bedding, and a muted yet earthy color palette. The standard room, known as the Andaz King, is roughly the same size as any other hotel room (but with far plusher amenities), while suites can get as large as over 900 square feet with deep bathtubs and dual-sided fireplaces. Downstairs, the Andaz Farmers Table restaurant serves relatively (at least for Napa) simple farm-to-table food that is tasty and filling.

Somewhere between a traditional B&B and a modern hotel like Andaz is **La Residence** (4066 Howard Ln., Napa, 707/253-0337 or 800/253-9203, www.laresidence.com, $250-400). It's actually more of a luxury country inn, with 25 guest rooms contained in four buildings set on two acres of wooded grounds with a hot tub and a small heated pool. The smallest and cheapest rooms are in the main mansion house, dating from 1870 and furnished with queen beds, original antiques, CD players, and TVs. Readers report that the plumbing in the old house can be temperamental, but all the bathrooms are nicely modernized. Larger (and more expensive) rooms in the more modern French Barn building have a touch of French country

style, plus balconies or patios and working fireplaces. The newest and biggest rooms are in the Cellar House, with LCD TVs, wet bars, and giant bathrooms added to the already long list of amenities. A couple of unique suites are similarly luxurious. Although the inn is nowhere near downtown Napa, it does offer easy access to the rest of the valley and is virtually next door to the excellent **Bistro Don Giovanni** (4110 Howard Ln., Napa, 707/224-3300, 11:30am-10pm Sun.-Thurs., 11:30am-11pm Fri.-Sat., dinner entrées $14-28). There is free wireless Internet access, a gourmet breakfast, and a casual reception every evening featuring wines from Hall winery.

There are luxurious resorts in the valley with views, others with wooded privacy, some with vineyards, but the **Milliken Creek Inn** (1815 Silverado Trail, Napa, 707/255-1197 or 800/835-6112, www.millikencreekinn.com, $450-650) has another twist—a riverside setting, an understated mix of Victorian and colonial Asian furnishings, relaxing earth tones, and the sense of exclusivity that comes from having just 12 guest rooms to share the lush gardens and fountains. All rooms come with full entertainment systems, luxurious linens, and wireless Internet access. The cheapest are the two Milliken rooms at $275-650, depending on the season and the time of the week. The premium rooms, starting at $450 a night (and going up to $875), include extras ranging from Jacuzzis and canopied beds to expansive private decks.

FOOD
River Front District and Downtown

"Global comfort food" is how the culinary creations at **Celadon** (500 Main St., Napa, 707/254-9690, www.celadonnapa.com, lunch 11:30am-2:30pm Mon.-Fri., dinner daily, dinner entrées $26) have been described, and the surroundings in the historic Napa Mill buildings are equally comfortable. The shabby-chic exterior and huge sheltered patio give way to a pure bistro-chic interior, the perfect match for the internationally influenced California menu.

The wine list offers about the same balance of California and the rest of the world.

At the other end of the mill is the pocket of Francophone charm **Angèle** (540 Main St., Napa, 707/252-8115, www.angelerestaurant.com, 11:30am-9pm Sun.-Thurs., 11:30am-10pm Fri.-Sat., $30). The rustic interior and canopied riverside patio are perfectly romantic settings for the classic French bistro food that has won plaudits from critics. Adding to its sophistication is an outstanding Californian and French wine list that includes about a dozen wines available by the half bottle.

Sake in Wine Country? Not a bad idea, particularly if it is paired with a dinner at **Morimoto's** (610 Main St., Napa, 707/252-1600, www.morimotonapa.com, 11:30am-2:30pm and 5pm-10pm Sun.-Thurs., 11:30am-2:30pm and 5pm-11pm Fri.-Sat., $25-40). The celebrity chef, Masaharu Morimoto, has appeared on the *Iron Chef* and recently relocated from New York to Napa to open this esoteric, sleek Japanese eatery. You won't find anything else like it in the Napa Valley, and it's not just its sake-leaning ways. The highly designed interior has a steel palette highlighted by bright yellow accents, and the food offers some traditional Japanese dishes, but all with a unique and modern twist. Gyoza with bacon cream, oyster foie gras, and duck confit fried rice are just a few menu items to confound any diner. There are also a handful of non sequiturs like steak, lobster, and roasted fingerling potatoes that add to the confusion. To get a full idea of the chef's culinary vision, order the tasting menu ($120). It's an adventure!

Another new addition is **The Pear** (720 Main St., Napa, 707/256-3900, 11:30am-9pm Sun.-Thurs., 11:30am-10pm Fri.-Sat.), a 50-seat bistro specializing in farm-to-table fare from New Orleans and the Deep South. This is not the place for haute cuisine or exploring the *terroir* of an onion. Instead, what you'll get are big plates of fried chicken, bourbon barbecue ribs, and standout dishes like shrimp creole pasta. In fact, after some time in Wine Country, this large-plate Southern comfort food may be just what the doctor ordered. Still, the low lighting,

open kitchen, and, of course, the wine list remind you that are in Napa, which is not a bad thing.

Trade in big plates for small plates and you get **ZuZu** (829 Main St., Napa, 707/224-8555, www.zuzunapa.com, lunch 11:30am-2:30pm Mon.-Fri., dinner 4:30pm-10pm Mon.-Thurs., 4:30pm-11pm Fri., 4pm-11pm Sat., 4pm-9:30pm Sun., plates $5-13), a refreshingly down-to-earth tapas bar that's a great place to end a stressful day of touring without having to worry about reservations or the bill. The cozy interior with its exposed brick, beams, and tile is the perfect setting for the Spanish-inspired small plates, none of which (except the Moroccan glazed lamb chops) costs over $12.

Downtown Joe's American Grill and Brewhouse (902 Main St., Napa, 707/258-2337, http://downtownjoes.com, 8:30am-10pm daily, dinner entrées $9-21) is a hopping alternative to the swanky restaurants and endless wine of the Napa Valley. Sure, it has a wine list (a short one), but most people come here for the more than half-dozen microbrews with the usual comical microbrew names, like Tantric India Pale Ale and Catherine the Great Imperial Stout. The menu is pretty standard if slightly pricey grill fare, but there's also a cheaper pizza and pub-grub menu to enjoy on the outside patio overlooking the river. There is live music in the evening Thursday-Sunday.

Equally local and down home is ◖ **Bounty Hunter Wine Bar and Smokin' BBQ** (975 1st St., Napa, 707/226-3976, www.bountyhunterwinebar.com, 11am-10pm Sun.-Thurs., 11am-11pm Fri.-Sat., plates and entrées $6-18), a wine shop, tasting bar, and barbecue joint. The setting, in a historic brick-walled Victorian building with knotty wood floors, a copper ceiling, and wine barrels for table bases, is as relaxed as the comfort food served. The menu includes gumbo, beer-can chicken (a Cajun-spiced chicken impaled on a Tecate beer can), and chili. Alternatively, just order some cheese and settle down at the wine bar with one of the 400 wines sold here (40 by the glass) or a tasting flight. Since it's a wine shop too, you'll pay retail prices for wines bought with a meal, and there'll be plenty of advice available from the fun-loving staff.

Those craving some hearty Italian food have several choices. **Ristorante Allegria** (1026 1st St., Napa, 707/254-8006, www.ristoranteallegria.com, lunch 11:30am-2:30pm and dinner 5pm-9pm daily, dinner entrées $20) is a cozy, leafy oasis tucked into a corner of the First Street Plaza, housed in a historic Italianate bank building that creates an air of Old World elegance. The restaurant is far larger than the exterior suggests, however, and can get noisy inside, so reserving a table on the small patio bordering the plaza is recommended. There's nothing terribly inventive about the menu, and the dining experience is not quite up to par with some of the more famous Italian restaurants up-valley, but with reasonable prices, a huge wine list, and competent cooking, it's a solid choice.

Uva Trattoria (1040 Clinton St. at Brown St., Napa, 707/255-6646, www.uvatrattoria.com, 11:30am-9pm Tues., 11:30am-9:30pm Wed.-Thurs., 11:30am-11:30pm Fri., 5pm-11:30pm Sat., 5pm-9pm Sun., $20) has become a Napa institution for its rustic Italian food and lively bar, and as one of the few live music venues in the city.

The best pizza in town can be found at **Azzurro Pizzeria & Enoteca** (1260 Main St., Napa, 707/255-5552, www.azzurropizzeria.com, 11:30am-9:30pm Mon.-Wed. and Sun., 11:30am-10pm Thurs.-Sat., $15, pizzas $13-17). The thin-crust pizzas from the wood-fired oven are some of the best in this part of the world—not surprising considering the founder of this popular restaurant honed his pizza skills at the famous Tra Vigne restaurant in St. Helena. The menu includes classic Italian starters, salads, and a handful of pasta dishes alongside the dozen or so pizzas, and there are plenty of choices for vegetarians. The wine list is dominated by thoughtfully chosen Napa and Sonoma wines, yet another sign that this is a no-nonsense and hassle-free dining experience favored by locals.

Oxbow Public Market

Want to try a bit of this and a bit of that? Venture across the river to the **C Oxbow Public Market** (610 and 644 1st St., Napa, 707/226-6529, www.oxbowpublicmarket.com, 9am-7pm daily). Showcasing local artisanal food suppliers and local restaurants, it is designed along the same lines as the highly successful Ferry Building Marketplace in San Francisco, which quickly became a magnet for the city's foodies after it opened in 2003. Oxbow, on a smaller scale, has a similar mix of restaurants and food vendors in a farm stand-like setting and is a one-stop shop for anyone looking for a quick fix of Napa Valley cuisine. Most of the tenants in the market are generally open at least 10am-7pm weekdays and 10am-6pm on weekends, but many are open later, as noted below.

Some of the restaurants that anchor the new development include outposts of St. Helena's gourmet burger joint **Gott's Roadside** (707/224-6900, http://gotts.com, 7am-9pm or 10pm daily)—formerly Taylor's Automatic Refresher—together with popular bakery and café **Model Bakery** (707/259-1128, http://themodelbakery.com, 6:30am-6:30pm Mon.-Fri., 7am-7pm Sat., 7am-6:30pm Sun.). Another interesting addition to the Napa food scene that has proven to be very popular is **Pica Pica Bar** (707/251-3757, www.picapicabar.com, 10am-8pm Sun.-Thurs., 10am-9pm Fri.-Sat.), said to be one of the first restaurants in California to offer Venezuelan street cuisine, which is known for its unique combinations of sweet and savory flavors, such as shredded skirt steak with black beans, cheese, and sweet plantains. The specialty dish is *arepas*, a corn flour-based flatbread filled with your choice of almost a dozen savory fillings and grilled to a crisp. Two other bread options are also offered, and all cost $8-9.

Another excellent south-of-the-border option is the innovative **C Casa** (707/226-7700, http://myccasa.com, 8am-9pm daily). Flavorful tacos of buffalo, spiced lamb, and citrus prawns compete with bi rotisserie plates of herb-crusted chicken and duck. Meanwhile, **Ca' Momi** (707/257-4992, www.camomienoteca.com,

7:30am-9pm daily) nearby serves perfect pizzas from the wood-fired oven, along with a healthy list of Italian (for a change) wines.

Restaurants are only half the story at Oxbow, however. One of the biggest draws is the cornucopia of Napa Valley food, from organic ice cream and olive oil to cheese and meats. **Five Dot Ranch** (707/224-5550, www.fivedotranch.com) sells every cut of grass-fed beef and every other meat imaginable, while the **Oxbow Cheese & Wine Merchant** (707/257-5200, 9am-9pm Tues.-Sat., 9am-8pm Sun.-Mon.) is a pungent tribute to local artisanal cheese makers. There's also an outpost of Sonoma's **Olive Press** (707/226-2679, www.theolivepress.com, 9am-7pm Mon. and Wed.-Thurs., 9am-8pm Tues. and Fri.-Sat., 9am-6pm Sun.) and more meats at the charcuterie **The Fatted Calf** (707/256-3684, www.fattedcalf.com) at the side of the market on McKinstry Street. Finish shopping or dining with a delectable organic dessert from **Three Twins Ice Cream** (707/257-8946, www.threetwinsicecream.com) or one of everyone's favorite treats from **Kara's Cupcakes** (707/258-2253, www.karascupcakes.com), which is hard to miss at the front of the main market building thanks to its giant pink menu board.

Vicinity of Napa

A little upriver, and certainly upscale, from the Oxbow Market is **La Toque** (1314 McKinstry St., Napa, 707/257-5157, www.latoque.com, 5pm-9pm daily, tasting menu $74-90). The Michelin-starred restaurant of the Westin Napa Verasa hotel gives Napa a touch of the Michelin magic felt farther north. Like you would expect, the food is French inspired, but generally less fussy and over the top than, say, at the French Laundry or Meadowood. But what really makes La Toque stand apart is the Truffle Menu of four savory courses, a cheese course, and dessert: all of which are centered around different truffles sourced from France and Italy. Such an experience will only set you back $200. If La Toque is slightly out of your range, try grabbing a table at the **Bank Café and Bar** (707/257-5151, 7am-2am daily $15),

La Toque's affordable sibling. This stylish alternative serves everything from breakfast to late-night bar snacks.

A few miles north of downtown Napa is the popular Italian restaurant **Bistro Don Giovanni** (4110 Howard Ln., Napa, 707/224-3300, 11:30am-10pm Sun.-Thurs., 11:30am-11pm Fri.-Sat., dinner entrées $14-28). It's hard to miss on the east side of Highway 29 (though you might miss the turn for Howard Lane) and is a favorite of locals looking for moderately priced Italian bistro food with a bit of California flair, all in a relaxed and vibrant setting. On a warm summer night, ask for a table on the huge bustling outdoor patio. Anything from the wood-fired oven is worth trying here, especially the pizzas and oven-roasted fish. The wine list is dominated by Napa and Sonoma, but there's a good choice from the mother country too, and an unusually wide selection by the half bottle.

If the relentless Wine Country-themed activities and food gets to be a bit too much, you can escape it all at the **Red Hen Cantina** (4175 Solano Ave., Napa, 707/255-8125, 10:30am-9pm Sun.-Thurs., 10:30am-9:30pm Fri.-Sat., entrées under $12), a colorful and sometimes raucous Mexican bar and restaurant right off Highway 29. Just look for the giant red hen on the roof of the building; it used to grace a nearby barn containing an antiques store. The food is by no means gourmet, and the bar can get packed, but if you stick to basics on the menu like enchiladas or a burrito, have a margarita or two, and sit out on the patio, you'll have an experience that is refreshingly devoid of Wine Country pretension.

Picnic Supplies

If you're in Napa and heading to the hills for lunch, the **Napa General Store** (540 Main St., Napa, 707/259-0762, 8am-6pm daily) in the Napa Mill complex is about as gourmet as you can get for take-out food in town. You'll have to battle your way past all the other nonfood trinkets and gifts it sells, though. At the **Oxbow Public Market** (610 and 644 1st St., Napa, 707/226-6529, www.oxbowpublicmarket.com,

9am-7pm daily), there are plenty of options for take-out food, from Pica Pica's Venezuelan food to gourmet sandwiches from the Model Bakery or The Fatted Calf charcuterie.

Just south of the Darioush winery is the **Soda Canyon Store** (4006 Silverado Trail, at Soda Canyon Rd., Napa, 707/252-0285, www.sodacanyonstore.com, 6am-6pm Mon.-Sat., 7:30am-5pm Sun.), just about the only decent place to buy deli food, cheeses, and wine along the Silverado Trail.

Farmers Market

Located next to the Oxbow Market, appropriately enough, the **Napa Downtown Market** (500 1st St., 707/501-3087, www.napafarmersmarket.com, 8am-12:30pm Tues. and Sat. May-Oct.) sells farm-fresh produce, along with local meat, cheese, and bread, and also has craft stalls.

INFORMATION AND SERVICES

First stop for any visitors without a plan—whether staying in Napa, heading up to Calistoga, or simply doing some online research—should be the **Napa Valley Welcome Center** (600 Main St., 707/251-5895, Napa, www.napavalley.org/nvcvb.html, 9am-5pm daily). The staff knows the valley like the backs of their hands and can usually rustle up some useful printed information. You'll also find tasting discounts dropped off by local wineries.

For current events, *Wine Country This Week* (www.winecountrythisweek.com) has the best up-to-date information. It can be found at most tasting rooms throughout Wine Country, and, as a casual read, it helps to get a feel for the valley. If it's local news you're seeking, you can find it in the daily *Napa Valley Register* (www.napanews.com).

Napa has a **post office** (1351 2nd St., 707/255-0621). For medical treatment (including alcohol poisoning), the **Queen of the Valley** (1000 Trancas St., Napa, 707/252-4411, www.thequeen.org) has both a 24-hour emergency room/trauma center and a by-appointment urgent-care clinic.

GETTING THERE AND AROUND

Coming from the south, Napa is the first city on Highway 29, just past the Highway 121 intersection. Its size makes it hard to miss, but the numerous exits can be confusing. Just keep your eyes peeled for the 1st Street exit, which leads straight to downtown, Oxbow Public Market, the Silverado Trail, and Coombsville beyond. Unless you're a local, you're not likely to need another exit. Once downtown, it is fairly easy to park either on the street or in relatively cheap public lots.

If you are considering going by bus, either to Napa or getting around once you're there, the **VINE** bus (800/696-6443, http://nctpa.net, adults $1.50-5.50, children $1-2.50) will take you where you need to go. Check the website for routes and schedules.

If the bus doesn't get you where you need to be (or at least in a timely manner, exploring Napa by bike is also easy. **Napa River Velo** (680 Main St., Napa, 707/258-8729, www.naparivervelo.com, 10am-6pm Mon.-Wed., 10am-7pm Thurs.-Fri., 9am-6pm Sat., 10am-5pm Sun.) is on the river side of the new Riverside Plaza development near the Napa Mill and rents bikes in the city of Napa for $35-75 per day, depending on whether you want a basic hybrid or a fancy road or mountain bike.

Yountville and Vicinity

While the **Yountville** name certainly goes far in the food world, you'll seldom see it mentioned on bottles, and the appellation certainly lacks the cachet of the hilly region to its east and the reputation for muscular cabs to the north. Still, Yountville can be relied on to produce tannic cabernets that age well in the bottle, as well as being cool enough for growing many other varietals, particularly chardonnay, sangiovese, zinfandel, sauvignon blanc, and even some pinot noir. Although wines from the Yountville AVA are certainly worthy of the Napa Valley pedigree, there is no one particular trait for which they are known.

A trip down the Silverado Trail would not be complete without visiting at least one of the two wineries that share the name of one of the best-known Napa appellations—one that helped put California on the international wine map in the 1970s. The **Stags Leap District** appellation on the eastern side of the valley along the Silverado Trail is perhaps one of the most recognizable Napa AVAs to wine lovers, particularly red-wine lovers. This fairly cool, hilly 1,300 acres of land rising up to the mountain crags (across which the legendary stag leapt to escape its hunters) is without doubt the land of cabernet sauvignon, and few other varietals get a look in. The cabernets have been famously described by the founder of Stag's Leap Wine Cellars as "an iron fist in a velvet glove," and they certainly have a gentle elegance that belies their sometimes astonishing aging potential. The combination of volcanic soils and cool air channeled between the handful of knolls that make up the district are thought to play a role in making this such a good place to create some of Napa Valley's best cabernets. Despite the fame of the Stags Leap District, most wineries here are refreshingly low-key.

YOUNTVILLE WINERIES
DOMAINE CHANDON
Crossing Highway 29, via underpass, on California Drive leads you to **Domaine**

Chandon winery (1 California Dr., Yountville, 707/944-2280, www.domainechandon.com, 10am-5pm daily, tasting $18-32), one of California's first big champagne houses and still one of the most impressive wineries in terms of architecture and landscaping. The buildings blend into the hillside beneath towering trees next to a giant (if slightly murky) pond and are almost invisible from the road. It's not the sort of modesty that one expects from such a big, glamorous operation producing several hundred thousand cases of sparkling and still wines each year; the surroundings are more earth-mother than youthful bling.

Once across the bridge and into the cavernous reception, skip the PR presentations and head upstairs to the spacious tasting bar and salon, with its cozy club-like atmosphere and doors out onto a leafy terrace and lawn area. Art is everywhere, both inside and out in the gardens, and you can buy pieces from some of the ever-changing exhibitions. The basic half-hour tour, which costs $15, takes in all stages of champagne making but runs only once daily at 1pm. For an additional $18, you can combine the tour with a tasting of both still and sparkling wines.

The tastings alone start at $18 (free glass included) for the Classic flight that includes the popular bone-dry Riche and some lower-end bubblies. For slightly more, the Prestige flight ($20) includes the more expensive vintage brut and Étoile sparklers that are bottle-aged for years to give them a rich, toasty aroma.

If you plan to take home a bottle or two, some of the reserve wines offer perhaps the best bargains, with far more complexity than the nonreserve wines for not much more money. Domaine Chandon also makes still wines from the three most important champagne grapes— pinot noir, chardonnay, and petit meunier. They're a little overpriced but worth trying if champagne is not your thing. All can be tasted as part of the Varietal flight ($22).

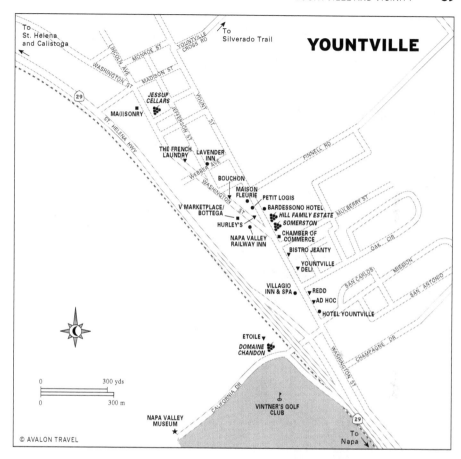

Unless you are into some serious champagne, however, pick the Classic tasting flight and kick back on the terrace with one of the tasty, if meager, appetizers. The terrace and the sometimes energetic atmosphere are as much reasons to come here as the champagne. Another big draw is the acclaimed restaurant, Étoile, which is as unashamedly high-end and stylish as the champagnes with which it shares the name. Gold cards and restrained elegance are the themes at this destination eatery—there is no written dress code, but you'll have a hard time getting beyond the concierge if you're wearing shorts.

Downtown Tasting Rooms

While there are relatively few wineries to visit in Yountville, more and more are opening tasting rooms on Washington Street. All are in easy walking distance; even Domaine Chandon, a full-fledged winery and a must-see, is an easy stroll from the heart of town.

MA(I)SONRY

At the top of Washington Street is perhaps the most unusual tasting room in the valley, **Ma(i)sonry** (6711 Washington St., Yountville, 707/944-0889, 10am-7pm daily, tasting $10-35). The space, located in a historic stone

© ELIZABETH LINHART VENEMAN

another side of Yountville

707/944-8523, www.jessupcellars.com, 10am-6pm daily, tasting $20). Like Ma(i)sonry, Jessup offers tastes of incredible boutique red wines you'll have a hard time finding anyplace else, but instead of high art, you get a cute little bar, a few shelves with items for purchase, and staff that love their jobs. If you chat them up, you may find yourself tasting rare Jessup vintages that are not on the usual list.

HILL FAMILY ESTATE

A few doors down from Jessup Cellars is the **Hill Family Estate** (6512 Washington St., Yountville, 707/944-9580, www.hillfamilyestate.com, 10am-6pm daily, tasting $20) tasting room, which also doubles as an antiques shop. Roam among the pricey French antiques as you sip, or take a seat on one of the lush leather couches. If you stand at the bar, you'll enjoy the company of the Hill family, who love to chat up customers tasting the small selection of light, balanced red and white wines. The cabernet sauvignons are not made in the typical heavy-handed Napa style, so even tasters with delicate palates will find them drinkable. Ask about the Double Barrel Cab, which is sold in a box that the younger sons of the winery have blasted full of buckshot with their grandfather's double-barrel shotgun.

SOMERSTON

A little bit of the Vaca Mountains can be found at the southern end of Washington Street at **Somerston** (6490 Washington St., Yountville, 707/944-8200, www.somerstonwineco.com, 1pm-8pm Sun.-Wed., noon-9pm Thurs.-Sat., tasting $10). Here, oversized photos of sheep grazing on mountain slopes, tables made of reclaimed wood, funky artistic flourishes, and exposed dark wood beams are the perfect setting for tasting their wines. The Highflyer wines are made from grapes grown from around the state and are the most affordable. The Somerston and Priest Ranch are largely estate wines sourced from the ranch vineyards, 2,800 feet above sea level deep in the mountains, photos of which grace the tasting room. These generally score high

building, showcases high-dollar art and high-end furnishings, and is home to a winery collective that pours flights from more than two dozen different small boutique wineries. With the exception of one Argentinean winery, all hail from California, if not Napa and Sonoma Counties. These are wines that you are unlikely to find anywhere else, as many of those featured only produce 300 cases or less. Tastings are seated with a "wine specialist," and appointments are necessary, particularly on weekends during the high season. Walk-ins are welcome, however, and the staff will try to accommodate you. Another option is to simply drink wine by the glass. Again, the list is long and the prices vary (the cheapest glass averaging around $9), but you still get to enjoy some superb wine surrounded by fine art and cutting-edge design.

JESSUP CELLARS

It's hard to miss the large stucco and exposed-beam building that is home to **Jessup Cellars** (6740 Washington St., Yountville, with the critics. Cheese and small bites are available to nibble while you taste, and if you would like to try some of the reserve wines, you can make an appointment for a seated tasting ($25-45).

Wineries by Appointment
BELL WINE CELLARS
If you want to spend some time with people who really know their wines, consider making a reservation at **Bell Wine Cellars** (6200 Washington St., Yountville, 707/944-1673, www.bellwine.com, 10am-4pm daily by appointment, tasting $20). The cab from Baritelle Vineyards in Rutherford, Bell's signature wine since 1991, is famous for being the valley's first-ever single-vineyard cabernet made from just one clone of the vine. Clone 6 cabernet is one of a handful of cabs made here that together account for the majority of the 10,000-case production. True cabernet lovers might want to splurge on the $125 clonal tasting, which includes cheese and a chance to try to distinguish the characteristics of four wines each made from a distinct clone of cabernet, including the clone 6 version.

Bell has also made a name for its syrah, sourced from the Sierra Foothills, and offers a couple of reasonably priced red blends, including a classic cabernet-based claret that understandably sells out fast considering its quality and modest $30 price. Whites are represented by Yountville chardonnay, a Lake County sauvignon blanc, and a pinot gris from Oregon's Willamette Valley. For $20 you'll taste five of Bell's current-release wines, but for $10 more the Grape to Glass tour will get you out into the vineyards, a barrel tasting, plus the five current-release wines paired with cheese. It's a good deal, but the drawback is that it starts at 10:30am

GOOSECROSS CELLARS
Anyone lamenting that everything wine-related in the Napa Valley costs too much should head on over to **Goosecross Cellars** (1119 State Ln., Yountville, 707/944-1986 or 800/276-9210, www.goosecross.com, 10am-4:30pm daily,

tasting $15). Producing only about 9,000 cases of wine, it is one of the valley's smaller wineries open to the public, and the laid-back family vibe is refreshing, especially considering its location. Plus, the standard tasting fee here is only $15, which is half what you'd pay at most nearby wineries.

The cozy tasting room is squeezed in next to the barrels and offers all 10 wines that this family-owned winery makes, including the standout Howell Mountain cabernet sauvignon and the crisp but fruity Napa Valley chardonnay. The flagship wine is the Aeros, a powerfully flavored red blend made only in the best vintages. From the minimal metal-winged label this is clearly a special wine, and chances are you won't be able to taste it because only a couple of hundred cases are made of each vintage. It's worth looking out for, nevertheless. Technically, Goosecross is appointment only thanks to county regulations, but if as a small group you roll up unannounced, you won't be turned away.

STAGS LEAP WINERIES
CLOS DU VAL
Although it has long since become a well-known Stags Leap District winery, **Clos Du Val** (5330 Silverado Trail, Napa, 707/259-2200 or 800/993-9463, www.closduval.com, 10am-5pm daily, tasting $15-30) is said to have come about because Bernard Portet, a Frenchman, wanted to make wines that rivaled Bordeaux. Established in 1972, Clos Du Val has succeeded. But driving up, you'll notice that the rather plain, concrete winery building itself seems to take more inspiration from 1970s design aesthetics than a Bordeaux château, illustrating that the showmanship here is definitely in the wines rather than the buildings or interior.

Almost half the wine made here each year is cabernet sauvignon, and this is the wine Clos Du Val is best known for. The generic Napa cabernet is good, but the Stags Leap estate cabernet is outstanding and comes from the vineyard right outside the winery door. Chardonnay is the other large-production wine in the portfolio and comes from the Carneros vineyard, as does a pinot noir. Another estate wine worth trying is the white Bordeaux blend of semillon and sauvignon blanc called Ariadne.

Tours are available daily by appointment only at 10:30am and 2:30pm. The $30 price tag includes a tasting of the Classic, Winemaker's Signature, and Reserve portfolio, making it well worth it. Or you can spend $5 and reserve a picnic table. On sunny Saturdays (which is often), the winery sets up a tasting bar out on the lawn, so you don't have to walk too far from your picnic spot or interrupt your game of *pétanque,* the French version of bocce, to try another wine.

STAG'S LEAP WINE CELLARS

The most famous winery of the AVA is **Stag's Leap Wine Cellars** (5766 Silverado Trail, Napa, 866/422-7523, www.cask23.com, 10am-4:30pm daily, tasting $15-30), which made the cabernet sauvignon that beat out the best French Bordeaux in the now-famous 1976 blind tasting in Paris, and followed it up with another win in the anniversary tasting 30 years later in 2006. It still makes outstanding single-vineyard cabernet from that same SLV vineyard as well as the older Fay vineyard next to it. Such renowned wines command high prices, none more so than the Cask 23 cabernet, which retails at about $210.

These three estate cabernets, together with an equally impressive chardonnay, can be tasted for $30. Non-estate wines from other Napa vineyards offer a cheaper tasting option ($15) and might include the excellent Artemis cabernet, the merlot, or the sauvignon blanc (you might also be able to steal a taste of these non-estate wines if you indulge in the more expensive tasting option). Appointment-only tours ($40) take in the pristine-looking cave system and its fascinating Foucault pendulum (for measuring the earth's rotation), and conclude with the estate tasting.

Although a magnet for serious wine enthusiasts, this family-run winery exudes an unassuming and friendly atmosphere, making it far less intimidating for the casual day-tripper than many of the valley's other big names. The small tasting room is off to the left of the main winery building and can get crowded, so plan to get here early.

PINE RIDGE WINERY

Nestled in a small dell with its trademark ridge of pine trees above is another of the Stags Leap District's big cabernet houses, **Pine Ridge Winery** (5901 Silverado Trail, Napa, 800/575-9777, www.pineridgewinery.com, 10:30am-4:30pm daily, tasting $20-40), one of the few wineries to make highly rated wines from most of Napa's finest cabernet appellations—Stags Leap, Rutherford, Oakville, and Howell Mountain.

The smallish tasting room is virtually devoid of merchandise, putting the wines firmly center stage as long as a tour bus has not just disgorged its passengers. The regular tasting option ($20) covers the white wines and cheaper reds, and might include a Carneros- or Rutherford-sourced chardonnay, viognier, merlot, or petit verdot. Appropriately enough there is an Appellation Tasting ($40) that includes wine from the various featured Napa Valley AVAs. Tours of the vineyard and aging caves, followed by a barrel tasting with cheese accompaniment, are offered three times a day by appointment (10am, noon, and 2pm, $50), and there's a small picnic area under the trees above the winery.

ROBERT SINSKEY VINEYARDS

It might be part of the elite group of Stags Leap wineries, but **Robert Sinskey Vineyards** (6320 Silverado Trail, Napa, 707/944-9090, www.robertsinskey.com, 10am-4:30pm daily, tasting $25-50), with its elegant stone and redwood exterior and lofty cathedral-like tasting area, is a feast for the senses in many different ways. Visitors are greeted by a field of lavender, an organic vegetable garden, and parking lot arbors covered in aromatic jasmine. The spacious tasting bar and demonstration kitchen are in the slender, tall main room that's reminiscent of a cathedral nave.

Robert Sinskey was one of the valley's earliest champions of organic farming. In 2007, the winery went a step further and was certified biodynamic, which explains the sheep photos you see around the winery. To boot, Rob Sinskey's wife, Maria, is a well-known chef and author of one of the better Napa Valley cookbooks, *The Vineyard Kitchen.*

In fact, food is as important as wine here. The demonstration kitchen at the back of the tasting room is a key stop on the Farm to Table tour ($75), offered by appointment at 11am daily. Picnicking is an option here, and at the tasting bar there are always morsels of food to accompany the wines, to illustrate the food-friendliness of the wines, and perhaps to make the relatively high tasting fees easier to swallow.

The wine that Robert Sinskey Vineyards is best known for is pinot noir, and there are three versions, all from Carneros—two from single vineyards and a slightly cheaper blend. Carneros vineyards are also the source of the merlot, cabernet, and cabernet franc that go into the elegant, Bordeaux-like Vineyard Reserve, a wine that tastes like it should cost far more than its sub-$40 price tag (which is why it usually sells out fast). Sinskey also makes some nice white pinots, including an unoaked pinot blanc and a heady Alsace blend of pinot gris, pinot blanc, riesling, and gewürztraminer called Abraxas. The Stags Leap District is represented by the estate cabernet sauvignon, which is every bit as good as wines from Sinskey's neighbors.

Wineries by Appointment
SHAFER VINEYARDS
Tasting wine at **Shafer Vineyards** (6154 Silverado Trail, Napa, 707/944-2877, www.shafervineyards.com, sales 9am-4pm weekdays, tasting 10am and 2pm weekdays by appointment, $45) is about as close as many visitors might get to one of Napa's much-hyped cult wines without forking over hundreds of dollars for the rare bottles that do make it beyond the waiting lists. Shafer's limited-production Hillside Select cabernet sauvignon is regularly compared to the highly extracted wines from

small producers like Screaming Eagle, Harlan Estate, and Bryant Family that are critically acclaimed and rare enough to command their cult status.

The secrets to success here are the rocky hillside vineyards behind the modest winery, which produce limited quantities of powerfully flavored grapes that go into the Hillside Select cabernet. Some of these grapes also make it into the lower-priced but equally plush cabernet. The winery also makes a chardonnay and merlot.

An informative sit-down discussion and tasting is offered twice a day on weekdays by appointment only, but the $45 price tag is a bit steep considering a tour of the facility is no longer included. The price could be worthwhile if the Hillside Select is available for tasting, but sometimes it has already sold out for the year. The consolation is that an excellent cabernet port that is only available at the winery usually is available for tasting. Space is limited to 10 people and demand is high, so booking weeks in advance is sometimes necessary, as is a tolerance of the serious oenophiles who tend to flock here. There's no sign for the winery on Silverado Trail, so look for the cluster of property numbers at the end of the private road almost opposite the entrance to Silverado Vineyards.

STAGS' LEAP WINERY
North on the Silverado Trail, down a long driveway lined with ancient walnut trees, is the first winery to bear the area's name, **Stags' Leap Winery** (6150 Silverado Trail, Napa, 800/395-2441, www.stagsleap.com, tour and tasting by appointment 10am and 2:30pm weekdays, $55). Its wines might be less famous than those of the other Stag's Leap, but its history and setting are far more impressive. The winery was founded in 1893, taking its name from the old Native American legend of a stag that evaded hunters by leaping across the craggy cliffs towering above the winery. The Victorian splendor remains fully intact today.

Perhaps the most noteworthy wines made here are the inky, full-bodied petite sirah and the proprietary Ne Cede Malis, a true Rhône-style field blend dominated by petite sirah that gets its name from the Latin phrase "Don't give in to misfortune," the motto of winery founder Horace Chase. Few people realize Stags' Leap is open to the public, but the appointment-only tours are available during the week for a limited number of people. They fill up fast, so book early. The tours take in the Manor House, winemaking facilities, and wonderful gardens including the apothecary, full of medicinal plants, and the sensory garden, devoted to flavorful and aromatic plants. Tie a visit here in with a tour of Shafer Vineyards, which shares the same driveway off the Silverado Trail.

SIGHTS

The history of Napa and the entire valley can be found at the **Napa Valley Museum** (55 Presidents Circle, Yountville, 707/944-0500, www.napavalleymuseum.org, 10am-4pm Tues.-Sun., adults $5, ages 17 and under $2.50). It usually has a fascinating mix of exhibits exploring the valley's natural and cultural heritage, from the modern wine industry back to Native American life, together with an interactive high-tech exhibit on the science of winemaking. The upstairs gallery provides space for rotating exhibitions, and you're likely to find the work of local artists or art depicting food and wine.

One new addition to this compact little town is the **Art Walk** (www.townofyountville.com) that stretches along Washington Street from California Street to Monroe Street. Since 2010, the town has been installing works of modern art from local and internationally known artists, and as of 2013, there were 30 installations in all. Look for the 200 stone mushrooms outside of the post office or the elegant *Great Blue Heron* hidden by the Vintage Inn. There are also plenty of rock and metal modern sculptures like Jedd Novatt's *Chaos Pamplona*, and *Belfry* by Napa's own Gordon Huether. The town's website has a printable map of the Art Walk, or you can pick one up at the **Yountville Visitors Center** (6484 Washington St., 707/944-0904, http://yountville.com, 10am-5pm daily).

If you want to extend your walk, pick up a Historical Walking Tour map also at the visitors center. Along the two-mile loop you'll see parks, the local pioneer cemetery, original Victorian homes, century-old storefronts, wineries, and much more. If you do the full loop and stop to admire the various sights, this walk may take you as much as 2-3 hours.

SHOPPING

Yountville (population about 3,000) is the little Napa Valley town that has become a big draw for diners and shoppers, with more restaurants per capita than seemingly any other place in the valley. Most of the action is in and around the giant brick **V Marketplace** building (6525 Washington St., Yountville, 707/944-2451, 10am-5:30pm daily) that was once a winery and distillery. It was built in 1870 by German immigrant Gottlieb Groezinger, who made most of his fortune decades earlier in the California gold rush.

The building has been tastefully restored inside, with the exposed brick and giant wooden beams lending an air of sophistication to the little boutique shops selling everything from clothes and accessories to toys, art, and the usual Wine Country gifts. Groezinger might turn in his grave if he saw it today, but not every shopping center can boast of being on the National Register of Historic Places.

Most of the stores clearly thrive on tourist dollars, but it's still fun to get lost for half an hour exploring the nooks and crannies of the three floors. Some of the more memorable shops include **Domain Home & Garden** (707/945-0222, www.domainhomeandgarden.com, 10am-5:30pm daily), which sells fun items for the home and garden, and **Napa Style** (707/945-1229, www.napastyle.com, 10am-5:30pm daily), just off the courtyard, which is a home chef's cornucopia and a slightly overdone homage to local celebrity chef Michael Chiarello—it's a challenge to find any item sold here that is not in some way branded with his name (a few steps away you can even eat at his newest restaurant, Bottega). Just across the courtyard is the **V Wine Cellar** (707/531-7053, www.vwinecellar.com, 10am-5:30pm daily), a decent and fairly large wine shop that sells a lot of local and international wines and has occasional tastings.

Arts and crafts lovers should cross Washington Street to the rather undistinguished and equally touristy **Beard Plaza,** which is where some of the town's galleries can be found, including **RAS Galleries** (707/944-9211, www.rasgalleries.com, 10am-5pm Wed.-Mon.), which features contemporary ceramic, glass, and sculpture artists. Another gallery hub is farther down Washington Street at the little plaza at the corner of Mulberry Street, also home to the Yountville Chamber of Commerce (6484 Washington St., Suite F, Yountville, 707/944-0904, www.yountville.com, 10am-5pm daily). Of particular note is the **Gordon Gallery** (6484 Washington St., 707/944-0823, http://thegordongallery.com, 10:30am-5:30pm Thurs.-Sun.), which specializes in truly lovely Napa Valley landscape paintings (oil and pastel). High-quality prints are also available.

If you're looking for more of an "art experience," head to the northern end of Washington Street, where art and design meets wine tasting at one of the most unique shopping experiences in the valley, **Maisonry** (6711 Washington St., 707/944-0889, 10am-7pm daily). Housed in a historic Victorian-era stone house, the concept for Maisonry is to be a living gallery, where the work of both contemporary and classical artists and designers is part of the decor and also happens to be for sale. The reality is that it can be a little intimidating stepping into such a rarefied atmosphere with its immaculately dressed staff, but just pretend you have several thousand dollars to blow and you'll quickly feel relaxed poking around the imaginative and beautifully made home furnishings and design pieces. There are a few reasonably priced items that would make good souvenirs of the Napa Valley, from antique wine bottles to Native American arrows, and the beautifully designed garden is a relaxing refuge in which to taste the many wines on offer.

RECREATION
Napa River Ecological Reserve
A small patch of land next to the river in Yountville has been saved from the vineyards, and it's now a great place to see wildlife other than the flocks of tourists more commonly sighted in these parts. Almost 150 types of bird and 40 types of butterfly call this peaceful 70-acre patch of the valley home. The reserve has no specific hours but is probably best avoided during the rainy season (Dec.-Apr.) when it can be too wet to be accessible.

The small paved parking lot is on the north side of Yountville Cross Road, about halfway between Highway 29 and the Silverado Trail, just west of the small bridge over the river. There's just one trail, about a mile long, that dives into woodland, crosses the river (only possible during the dry summer and fall months), and eventually loops back on itself, but not before affording a unique view of the valley's native wildlife and plant life.

Golf
Just south of the Domaine Chandon winery is the nine-hole, 2,800-yard **Vintner's Golf Club** (7901 Solano Ave., off California Dr., Yountville, 707/944-1992, www.vintnersgolfclub.com, call for tee times). Fees for nonresidents range from $20 midweek to $25 weekends for nine holes, and up to $35 to play 18 holes.

Spas
An easy walk from anywhere in downtown Yountville, the **Spa Villagio** (6481 Washington St., Yountville, 800/351-1133, 7:30am-9pm daily) has a beautiful space in which to pamper its patrons. You don't need to be a guest at the Villagio Inn to book a treatment at the spa, though you may wish for one of the five Spa Suites—private spaces where singles, couples, and friends can relax before, during, and after their treatments. Being the Napa Valley, you can even pair your treatment with wine and food bites for a $575, 3.5-hour luxury experience. Otherwise, massages run from $125-135 for 50 minutes and $250-270

for 100 minutes, while mud baths and other soaks cost $145 for 50 minutes and $250 for 100 minutes. But whatever your indulgence, be sure to show up an hour early for your massage, facial, or treatment package—at the price you're paying for treatments here, you'll definitely want to take advantage of the saunas and hot tubs, relaxation rooms, and all the other chichi amenities. The spa recommends making reservations for your treatment at least three weeks in advance, especially during the summer and fall seasons.

Another purely Napa Valley option is the 50-minute "Uncorked" treatment at the **North Block Spa** (6757 Washington St., 707/944-8080, http://northblockhotel.com/spa, 8am-8pm daily), in which for 60 or 90 minutes you may have your feet rubbed with ground grape seeds and pressure points massaged with wine corks. It will cost you $120 or $188, respectively, or for the same amount you can select one of the spa's other signature treatments, like the Stiletto Blues, which uses hot stone massage to heal well-heeled soles; a Hats Off scalp massage; and a massage designed just for Moms. The spa also offers acupuncture, facials, and dry exfoliation treatments in its modern and minimalist setting.

ACCOMMODATIONS

The small town of Yountville not only has an impressive number of restaurants and shops but also a lot of hotel rooms for its size. Being right next to Highway 29 and a major cross-valley road, it is within easy reach of just about every valley winery.

Those advantages make the town both blessed and cursed, however. Easy access and plentiful services make it a great base from which to explore the valley, but Yountville also attracts hordes of visitors during the day and suffers from almost constant traffic noise near Highway 29, destroying much of the rural charm and often making it feel more like a suburban mall than a historic town of 3,000 residents. You might wonder where all the locals actually are—they tend to emerge at night after the shops close.

$150-200

The Orient Express it is not, but this is the only place in the valley where you can sleep on a train. Sort of. The nine railcars and cabooses that constitute the affordable **Napa Valley Railway Inn** (6523 Washington St., Yountville, 707/944-2000, $125-260) took their last trip many decades ago and are now fitted out with king or queen beds, air-conditioning, skylights, flat-screen TVs, and private bathrooms, making surprisingly comfortable accommodations right in the middle of Yountville. The downside is that they are stranded in the middle of a sea of blacktop that is the parking lot for the V Marketplace (no problem parking here), and the inn is only staffed during daylight hours, with just an emergency number for any nighttime mishaps. The odd-numbered red rooms have nice views of vineyards and the hills beyond, if you can overlook the large parking lot and Highway 29. The blue rooms are a bit quieter and back onto a smaller parking lot and downtown Yountville. There's enough tall greenery planted to offer some privacy from late-night parkers, but it's still wise to remember to draw the curtains when it gets dark.

In the heart of Yountville is the ◖ **Maison Fleurie** (6529 Yount St., Yountville, 707/944-2056 or 800/788-0369, www.maisonfleurie-napa.com, $150-250), which also does its best to be more French than Californian. The old ivy-covered stone-and-brick buildings around a pretty courtyard certainly evoke the French countryside, as do the vineyards almost across the street (if you ignore the contemporary Bardessono Hotel that sprouted up next to the vines). Inside the cozy lobby and the 13 guest rooms the French country theme continues, though it tends to go a little over the top with the flowery fabrics and faux antiques. Cozy is also the word used by the hotel to describe its smallest and cheapest rooms—the Petite Full and the Petite Queen rooms are just 80 square feet. If you do get one, plan on spending time outside by the small pool to prevent claustrophobia. The biggest rooms are in the adjoining Carriage House and Bakery buildings and include fireplaces, views, and spa tubs in some.

The French theme continues (in name, at least) at the tiny **Petit Logis** (6527 Yount St., Yountville, 877/944-2332, www.petitlogis. com, $135-295), tucked away in a one-story building next to Maison Fleurie. The five rooms in a row of former shops have their own outside entrances and are decorated in fairly minimal but comfortable France-meets-New England country style. They include private bathrooms with whirlpool tubs. Unlike many places, breakfast is not included, but for an additional charge one can be arranged at a nearby restaurant by the hotel staff.

Over $200

The Yountville area has more than its fair share of upscale lodgings, many of which seem to be competing for conference and meeting business. That roughly translates to some slightly unjustified prices for the average visitor. Two that are probably more worth the top dollar they charge than most are Villagio Inn & Spa and Vintage Inn, large resort-style properties on either side of the V Marketplace shopping center that are spacious, luxurious, and far more service-oriented than lower-priced inns. The concierges are actually able to get reservations at the best local restaurants when your own attempts might fail.

The **Vintage Inn** (6541 Washington St., Yountville, 707/944-1112, www.vintageinn. com, $330-650) has a French theme and is the smaller and more attractive of the two, with rooms arranged around gardens, fountains, and pools. The **Villagio Inn & Spa** (6481 Washington St., 707/944-8877 or 800/351-1133, www.villagio.com, $340-675) has Tuscan-themed decor and similar amenities, plus an on-site spa (that can also be used by Vintage Inn guests), but it is in a cluster of buildings that looks like an extension of the neighboring apartment complex despite the faux Roman gardens. Neither Euro-theme is terribly convincing, but both inns have very similar spacious rooms with fireplaces, sunken tubs, and a small outdoor patio or balcony. Rates are similar at both properties and are determined in part by position.

The nine spacious rooms of the **Lavender Inn** (2020 Webber St., Yountville, 707/944-1388 or 800/522-4140, www.lavendernapa. com, $225-350) are themed in French country style, though with a little more of a contemporary feel. All have fireplaces, and a few have private hot tubs and patios to take in the smell of the lavender gardens on warm summer nights. Guests can use the pool at Maison Fleurie down the road.

If you're looking for some contemporary luxury with plenty of green cred, the sprawling **Bardessono Hotel** (6526 Yount St., Yountville, 707/204-6000, www.bardessono.com, $600-800) is the newest member of the Napa Valley's growing collection of super-resorts catering to those with money to burn for the ultimate in pampering. The 62-room hotel is one of only a few worldwide to be LEED-Platinum certified, thanks to a laundry-list of nature-friendly design and operational features, but its much-touted environmental credibility is dented somewhat when you consider the fact that part of the vineyard farmed by the Bardessono family for three generations was ripped out to build the place. Arranged around multiple courtyards with its own meandering streams, it resembles a contemporary luxury condo development more than a traditional hotel, but the amenities and services are what you'd expect when every room is a suite and costs upward of $600 per night—massive TVs, private patios, fireplaces, outdoor showers, giant Jacuzzi tubs, countless spa treatments, and the finest linens money can buy.

Adding to the list of high-end resort hotels is the **Hotel Yountville** (6462 Washington St., Yountville, 707/867-7900 or 888/944-2885, www.hotelyountville.com, $450). When the current owners decided to revamp the old Yountville Inn, they eschewed the modern steel, Swiss pearl siding, and Brazilian hardwood in favor of French farmhouse appeal that has been the cornerstone of the Yountville aesthetic. Adding 40 rooms to total 80, the entire hotel has cobblestone exterior, exposed beams, and tons of natural light. The standard rooms, or "Deluxe Rooms," and the slightly bigger "Premium Rooms" each have vaulted ceilings, a four-poster bed, white Italian linens, a fireplace, a spa tub, and French doors opening onto a private patio. Suites are also available, with all the same amenities but a lot more space. As you would expect, there is a full-service spa, a pool, and a high-end restaurant.

FOOD

Anchored by The French Laundry, Yountville has become something of a restaurant mecca in the Napa Valley in recent years as the town continues to transform itself and move further upmarket.

Downtown Yountville

Good luck trying to get a reservation at **The French Laundry** (6640 Washington St., Yountville, 707/944-2380, www.frenchlaundry.com, dinner 5:30pm-9pm daily, lunch 11am-1pm Fri.-Sun., reservation only, $270). The famous restaurant is usually booked up two months in advance thanks to its world renown, limited seating, and strict reservations system. Reservations can only be made two months in advance, and such is the demand that all the slots for the two evening seatings two months hence are usually snapped up the first morning they are made available. This is the case for much of the year, particularly on weekend nights and despite the astronomical price tag, so either be prepared to hit redial for the best part of a morning or persuade your hotel to make a reservation for you. If you are one of the lucky few to get in, you'll probably remember the seven- or nine-course prix fixe dinner as your best meal all year, but you'll want to forget the $270 price in a hurry. If you can't get a reservation, you can at least see some of the ingredients growing in the restaurant's own organic vegetable garden just across the street.

Touched by the same magic, however, is French Laundry's little cousin down the road, **Bouchon** (6534 Washington St., Yountville, 707/944-8037, www.bouchonbistro.com, 11:30am-midnight Mon.-Fri., 11am-midnight Sat.-Sun., $34), a French bistro that excels at *croque monsieurs* and *steak frites*. The

brief menu still evokes a relaxed Parisian hole, helped by a smattering of French wines on the otherwise Napa-dominated list. Reservations, while not necessary, are recommended. But, if you're just looking for a breakfast pastry or a sandwich, walk from Bouchon to the **Bouchon Bakery** (6528 Washington St., Yountville, 707/944-2253, www.bouchonbakery.com, 7am-7pm daily) next door. This ultra-high-end bakery supplies both Bouchon and The French Laundry with pastries and breads, as well as operating a retail storefront. Locals and visitors flock to the bakery at breakfast and lunchtime, so expect a line.

And then there is **Ad Hoc** (6476 Washington St., Yountville, 707/944-2487, dinner 5pm-10pm Thurs.-Mon., brunch 10am-1pm Sun., prix fixe menu $52), Thomas Keller's most recent adventure in Yountville. Ad Hoc aims for (and hits with a perfect bull's-eye) a rustic family style. The four-course menu changes nightly, and you'll get no choices, but considering the quality of the rustic seasonal fare, that's not necessarily a bad thing. The only certainty is that there'll be either soup or salad followed by a meat or fish main course, a cheese course, and dessert. The casual family-style dining suits the food better than the wine. The wine list is suitably endowed with moderately priced California and international wines, but markups are higher than is usual in this part of the wine world, and glasses are simple tumblers rather than stemware, which makes the prices even more egregious. Reservations are not quite as hard to get as at the Laundry, but don't expect to walk in and get a table most evenings either.

Next door to Ad Hoc is the sleek modern home of **Redd** (6480 Washington St., Yountville, 707/944-2222, www.reddnapavalley.com, lunch 11:30am-2:30pm Mon.-Sat., dinner 5:30pm-9:30pm daily, brunch 11am-2:30pm Sun., entrées $20-32), a critically acclaimed restaurant outside of the Keller constellation. The minimalist contemporary dining room oozes with luxurious fabrics, fixtures, and furniture, a style that is mirrored by the modern American cooking that has been compared favorably to the food at The French Laundry. If you're in the mood to splurge, the $80 five-course taster menu is well worth the price. On the other hand, a bacon-infused Bloody Mary ordered with the Hangtown Fry omelet and fried oysters is a perfect brunch after a late night of wining and dining.

If a visit to a Yountville restaurant is not complete without a celebrity chef sighting, make a reservation at **Bottega** (6525 Washington St. A9, Yountville, 707/945-1050, www.botteganapavalley.com, 5pm-9:30pm Mon., 11:30am-2:30pm and 5pm-9:30pm Tues.-Thurs. and Sun., 11:30am-2:30pm and 5pm-10pm Fri.-Sat., $15-30), where celebrity chef Michael Chiarello frequently strolls out into the dining room, wooing patrons. Aside from the finely executed Italian cuisine, the big draw here is the outside covered patio where two large fireplaces, ringed by couches, invite you to sip a cocktail or glass of wine late into the evening or on a rainy afternoon.

But if celebrity sightings are not your thing and you're hungry for a local favorite, **Bistro Jeanty** (6510 Washington St., Yountville, 707/944-0103, www.bistrojeanty.com, 11:30am-10:30pm daily, $26) just may be the place for you. The menu is a single page devoted to the classics of Parisian bistro cuisine. Tomato bisque served with a puff pastry shell, traditional salads, cassoulet, coq au vin, even a *croque monsieur* are all crafted with obvious joy. Every local Yountville resident will lovingly describe his or her own favorite dish. Service is friendly, and you'll see a few locals hanging at the bar, watching the TV tuned to a sports channel—something of a non sequitur here. Jeanty has two dining rooms, making walk-in dining easy on off-season weeknights, but definitely make a dinner reservation if you're in town on the weekend or in high season.

Along St. Helena Highway (Highway 29)

Étoile (1 California Dr., Yountville, 888/242-6366, www.chandon.com, 11:30am-2:30pm and 6pm-9pm Thurs.-Mon., $35) is a high-end restaurant not to be overshadowed by the esteemed eateries on the other side of the highway. It sits inside the tasting facility at the prestigious Domaine Chandon champagnery, overlooking Chandon's lush green gardens, with lovely white tablecloths that sparkle in the sunlight. The menu at Étoile is inventive even for Napa, and each dish is prepared to utter perfection. Order the chef's tasting menu ($95 for four courses) with wine pairings (an additional $70) to sample Chandon's wine list at its best and enjoy the delectable cuisine as it was intended to be eaten.

One of the first big roadside restaurants north of Napa is **Brix** (7377 St. Helena Hwy., Yountville, 707/944-2749, www.brix.com, 11:30am-9pm Mon.-Sat., 10am-2pm and 4:30pm-9pm Sun., entrées $19-34), a cavernous place with a little bit of an expense-account atmosphere but that serves some nicely executed French-inspired cuisine. A standout feature of the restaurant is the big patio overlooking vineyards, which is perhaps best enjoyed on Sunday mornings when the kitchen serves a gourmet brunch buffet (adults $38.50, kids 7-13 $18.50, 6 and under free) complete with artisan cheeses, salads, eggs, pizzas, and a seafood bar.

Mustards Grill (7399 St. Helena Hwy., Yountville, 707/944-2424, 11:30am-9pm Mon.-Thurs., Fri 11:30am-10pm, 11am-10pm Sat., 11am-9pm Sun., dinner entrées $17-26) is considered the king of the valley grills, having been around for over 25 years and having seen many more-fashionable restaurants in the valley come and go. Such longevity and fame, however, have also put it firmly on the tourist map, as illustrated by the line waiting for tables on busy weekends. It might not look like much from the outside and resembles a fancy roadhouse on the inside, but unlike the Rutherford Grill, which is now part of a chain, Mustards is a thoroughly Napa Valley affair, run by Cindy Pawlcyn, who also owns a couple of unique restaurants in St. Helena. It has spawned a cookbook and grows many of its own vegetables in its garden, as only a Napa restaurant could. The menu is filled with the sort of rich roasted and grilled meats that scream for a powerful Napa cabernet sauvignon, of which there are several dozen on the international wine list.

Picnic Supplies

In Yountville, the **Bouchon Bakery** (6528 Washington St., Yountville, 707/944-2253, www.bouchonbakery.com, 7am-7pm daily), opposite the V Marketplace, has a limited selection of very good sandwiches for under $10, as well as fresh bread and some sweeter bakery delights (try the macaroons). Right at the back of the **Napa Style** store, itself at the back of the V Marketplace, a small deli offers gourmet made-to-order sandwiches, although they tend to be on the pricey side. A limited selection of soft drinks is also available. Locals are usually to be found ordering lunch at the **Yountville Deli,** which is on the north side of the **Yountville Ranch Market** (6498 Washington St., 707/944-2002, 6am-10pm daily, deli 6am-3pm daily). A full range of sandwiches is available in the deli for $6-8 along with full box lunches ($13), and the market itself has everything else you might need for a picnic, from bread and cheese to beverages, including plenty of half bottles of local wine.

INFORMATION AND SERVICES

The tiny **Yountville Chamber of Commerce** (6484 Washington St., Ste. F, Yountville, 707/944-0904, www.yountville.com, 10am-5pm daily) is awash with guides, leaflets, magazines, and advice about the local area. The concierge desk at the **V Marketplace** shopping center is also worth stopping at for some local tips and information.

GETTING THERE AND AROUND

Yountville sits snuggly on Highway 29, just nine miles north of Napa. Downtown is on the east side of the highway, and Washington Street is its main corridor. Easily enough, Washington Street connects with Highway 29 at the south and north end of town, but to get to the heart of Yountville, exit on California Drive in the south and Madison Street in the north. The Yountville Cross Road will take you from the north end of town to the Silverado Trail. To get here via bus, jump aboard the **VINE** (800/696-6443, http://nctpa.net, adults $1.50-5.50, children $1-2.50), a commuter bus that runs from the East Bay up through Calistoga.

Another option, particularly after an indulgent meal, is the **Yountville Trolley** (707/944-1234, http://nctpa.net, 10am-2pm and 4pm-7pm Wed.-Fri., 10am-7pm Sat.-Sun., after 7pm pickup by request only, free). Running on a fixed track from Yountville Park, along Washington Street, to California Drive (conveniently near Domaine Chandon), the trolley is a cute historical ride through a cute historical town. It may also be a cheap and convenient way back to your hotel after imbibing a bit too much.

The Yountville area is great to explore by bike, particularly the Stags Leap District; a mile-long **bike trail** (www.vinetrail.org) opened in 2010 and runs the length of town, giving cyclists a break from navigating cars at least for a little while. **Napa Valley Bike Tours** (6795 Washington St., Bldg. B, Yountville, 707/251-8687, www.napavalleybiketours.com, 8:30am-5pm daily) offers rentals by the day, as well as customized Self-Guided Bike Tours ($89) that include a picnic lunch, wine purchase pickup, and van support. On their own, bike rentals run $39-65 per day. Electric hybrids are also available ($55/day), as well as tandem bikes ($78) and bike trailers for kids ($25). Loaner bikes at some of the posher hotels are increasingly coming into vogue, like at the **Hotel Yountville** (6462 Washington St., Yountville, 707/867-7900 or 888/944-2885, www.hotelyountville.com, $450), so be sure to ask about availability when making reservations or checking in.

Oakville and Rutherford

This is a part of the valley where the weather starts to get seriously warm in the summer, and the cabernets get seriously muscular. In fact, nearly 70 percent of the vineyards in this appellation are planted to cabernet sauvignon, and the area was home to some of the pioneering wineries in the Napa Valley.

Oakville begins just north of Yountville and stretches across the valley, earning its reputation from the sandy, well-drained soils. Here is where the land of big bold Napa cabernets begins in the valley, but the appellation also turns out some excellent sauvignon blanc and chardonnay. For this reason, it was also the home to some of the valley's famous wineries stretching back to the 1800s.

Like Oakville, **Rutherford** is a big appellation that spans the width of the valley. Some critics suggest there is not a great deal of difference between the two neighboring appellations—both have similar soils and weather, and both are capable of producing rich, muscular cabernets with exceptional balance. How Rutherford earned the bigger name over the years for cabernets might be partly due to the historic and influential wineries that made wine here, such as Inglenook and Beaulieu. Indeed, it was Beaulieu's famous winemaker, André Tchelistcheff, who made the connection between the distinctive soils of the region and their influence on the characteristics of the equally distinctive wines. "It takes Rutherford dust to grow great cabernet," he famously said.

You might also often hear the term "Rutherford Bench," a section of the AVA down the western side of the valley that is not benchland in the traditional sense and was never granted its own appellation status. It has become an oft-used marketing term nonetheless, normally used to suggest the best part of the Rutherford region.

East of Rutherford, hidden in oak-studded peaks and valleys of the Vaca Mountains is the slender **Chiles Valley AVA.** Grapes have been grown here for more than 100 years, and the area was ripe for a new wave of viticultural development until the valley's biggest growers recently turned their attention farther north to Lake County, where land is cheaper and the promised investment return greater. Nevertheless, there are still some great wines made in these hills, most notably zinfandel and sauvignon blanc, which enjoy the warmer growing conditions.

OAKVILLE WINERIES

NAPA WINE COMPANY

The modest Cellar Door tasting room of the **Napa Wine Company** (7830 Hwy. 29, Oakville, 800/848-9630, www.cultwinecentral.com, 10:30am-4:30pm daily, tasting $25), just across the road from the Oakville Grocery, does not suggest that this is a huge winemaking and grape-growing operation. The tasting room is a cooperative of 25 small wineries, and the Napa Wine Company itself, which manages to make about 10,000 cases of its own wine as well, including a highly regarded cabernet sauvignon.

Some of the small wineries represented in the tasting room have links to some major valley personalities, while others here are simply small or medium-sized family affairs, making a stop here the best way to taste some outstanding Napa Valley wines made without the usual Napa Valley fanfare. For the price of a tasting you can select 5 wines from the 10-wine menu.

ROBERT MONDAVI WINERY

This sprawling mission-style complex with its distinctive giant archway and bell tower is considered by some to be the temple of modern Napa winemaking, with the late Robert Mondavi the high priest. Others are of the opinion that it's a classic example of the overcommercialization of the Napa wine industry—and judging by the crowds and limos that throng the winery, they have a point. The **Robert Mondavi Winery** (7801 Hwy. 29,

Oakville, 888/766-6328, www.robertmondaviwinery.com, 10am-5pm daily) was once the crown jewel of the Mondavi Corporation, which started life in the 1960s, ushering in the valley's modern-day wine industry. Touring the impressive grounds and buildings and learning about their history and about winemaking are certainly the highlights of visiting the winery, and give the wines a lot to live up to. Despite the naysayers (and there are plenty), the wines are still rather special, particularly if you stick to the classic cabernet, chardonnay, and sauvignon blanc on which Mondavi has historically focused. Opportunities to taste more wines are somewhat limited.

The Signature Tour and Tasting ($25) includes a 30-minute stroll through the vineyards and winery and includes a tasting of three wines. You can usually sign up for a same-day tour at the reception desk. The number of other tours is quite bewildering, numbering almost a dozen in the summer, so check the website for options. Highlights include the Twilight Tour ($50), which is perfect for the end of a hot summer day; the Wine Basics tasting, which is a bargain at $20 for wine-tasting "beginners"; and the Discovery Tour, which is billed as good for parents with kids ($15), but only two wines are tasted. There are also options for cheese and chocolate pairing.

Without a tour the tasting options are limited to $5-15 per wine in the Le Marche tasting room or $40 for a flight of four reserve wines in the To Kalon Room. Of course, if the modern-day Napa Valley that Mondavi helped create has already bankrupted you, it's always free to wander around the courtyard to admire the architecture and views, and imagine a time in the 1960s when this was virtually the only winery in the area.

SILVER OAK

"Life is a Cabernet" is the motto of **Silver Oak** (915 Oakville Cross Road, Oakville, 707/942-7022, www.silveroak.com, 9am-5pm Mon.-Sat., 11am-5pm Sun., tasting $20-30). There are two Silver Oak wineries, this one in Napa Valley's Oakville and another in Geyserville in

Alexander Valley. Oakville is the home of the Napa Valley cabernet sauvignon and the original site of Silver Oak Cellars. The attractive grounds feature a courtyard, fountain, water tower, and the timber-framed tasting room. The interior of the tasting room and the winery's exterior are lined with limestone. Silver Oak is known for exceptional, food-friendly cabernet sauvignons. A significant portion of the website is devoted to foods that are enhanced by cabernet and to a lesser extent, Silver Oak's merlot, pinot noir, and sauvignon blanc. Winery chef Dominic Orsini focuses on creating menus, food pairings, and recipes that showcase the bold flavors of the wines. He describes his style as soulful Italian, and sources olives and fresh herbs from the winery's organic gardens. Visitors can make a reservation for a food pairing with Chef Orsini, book Silver Oak for a private event, or simply drop in for a taste of their current releases.

PLUMPJACK WINERY

Former two-term mayor of San Francisco and current lieutenant governor of California, Gavin Newsom is a busy guy. In addition to his public service duties, he is an entrepreneur and wine enthusiast who co-created his retail venue Plumpjack Wines with billionaire philanthropist Gordon Getty. This enterprise expanded to include **PlumpJack Winery** (620 Oakville Cross Road Oakville, 707/945-1220, www.plumpjackwinery.com, 10am-4pm daily, tasting $15) and other related ventures including wine shops, restaurants, bars, and resorts. Plumpjack's name is inspired by Sir John "PlumpJack" Falstaff, one of Shakespeare's most memorable comic foils. Newsom and Getty strive for approachable wines and a convivial attitude that's true to their namesake. Plumpjack was founded on the belief that wine is one of life's pleasures to be enjoyed as part of a complete dining experience. The winery itself dates back to the 1800s and is surrounded by a 42-acre estate vineyard. It's known for outstanding cabernet sauvignon. The winemaking team creates full-bodied, elegant wines that have earned PlumpJack critical acclaim, including an estate cabernet sauvignon, reserve cabernet sauvignon, reserve chardonnay, Napa Valley syrah and merlot.

Wineries by Appointment
OPUS ONE
Only serious wine lovers need go out of their way to visit **Opus One** (7900 Hwy. 29, Oakville, 707/944-9442, www.opusonewinery.com, 10am-4pm daily, tours 10:30am, tasting $40), the monolithic tribute to red Bordeaux that was formed in 1979 by Robert Mondavi and the late legendary French winemaker Baron Philippe de Rothschild, head of famed Château Mouton-Rothschild in France. In a valley filled with ever more bold architectural statements, the building housing this grand winery is still one of the most fascinating and looks like it will stand the architectural test of time.

This is a proudly appointment-only winery. The concierge escort to the tasting room and $40 tasting fee to taste just the single type of wine made here are reminders that Opus One was California's very first ultra-premium winery. It still tries hard to retain that edge with its attitude and its wines, including among the best cabernet in the valley. It's not a place for those easily intimidated by posh exclusivity. The tasting fee is made easier to swallow because it buys you virtually an entire glass of the current vintage of the signature wine, which retails for $160 a bottle, and gets you access to the rooftop terrace with its fantastic views. Opus One also makes a cheaper nonvintage cabernet called Overture that sells for about a third that price, not that you'll see much evidence of it at the winery.

The hour and a half tour and tasting ($60) is well worth taking if you can get a reservation. It takes in some of the striking features and technology of the building. Completed in 1991, the winery is a half-buried architectural tribute to the contemporary and old-school heritages (and wines) of the two founders, and from afar it resembles a giant limestone spaceship landed in the vineyards. Inside, antique European furniture blends with minimalist design touches and state-of-the-art winemaking elements like the giant semicircular barrel-aging room.

FAR NIENTE
One of Napa's most well-respected wineries, **Far Niente's** (1350 Acacia Dr., off the Oakville Grade, Oakville, 707/944-2861, www.farniente.com, tours by appointment 11am-3pm daily, $50) appointment-only tour and tasting is among the best in the valley. The winery makes only two highly regarded (and expensive) wines—cabernet sauvignon and chardonnay—so the tasting of five wines will always include some older library vintages. Despite the $50 price tag, the tour is extremely popular, and booking in advance during the summer is essential.

Far Niente was established as a winery in the late 1800s, and the name is Italian for "without a care." Far Niente (Italian for "without a care") was established as a winery in the late 1800s by Gil Nickel, who also founded the nearby Nickel and Nickel winery. Among the highlights of the history-laden tour are a walk through the aging caves under the main house, which have been extended into a 40,000-square-foot labyrinth over the decades, and a chance to see Nickel's classic cars in the Carriage House, many of which he raced at some point, including a rare prototype Ferrari known as the Yellow Beast. Those lucky enough to visit in April and May will also see some of the 8,000 azaleas in bloom in the 13 acres of gardens with a sweeping view of the valley.

NICKEL & NICKEL
Located almost opposite the lavish Mondavi winery is the rather quaint Victorian farmstead of **Nickel & Nickel** (8164 Hwy. 29, Oakville, 707/967-9600, www.nickelandnickel.com, tasting and tours by appointment 10am-3pm Mon.-Fri., 10am-2pm Sat.-Sun., $50), sister winery to Far Niente just down the road. Many of the buildings in the complex date from the late 1800s, but there is

also a cunningly disguised state-of-the-art winery hidden in the huge barn built recently using Victorian building methods. The barn sits atop a huge underground barrel room with vaulted ceilings that would make any Victorian engineer proud.

The collection of beautifully restored cottages and barns and the centerpiece 1884 Sullenger House can be seen on the appointment-only tour, a sedate and classy affair that culminates in the tasting of five of the wines. Although cabernet dominates the production, there are some outstanding chardonnays from Napa Valley and the Russian River Valley made in varying styles, as well as syrah, merlot, and zinfandel. Many of the wines here are 100 percent varietal wines (made entirely from one type of grape rather than containing small percentages of blending grapes that never get mentioned on the bottle).

RUTHERFORD WINERIES
PEJU PROVINCE WINERY
Peju (8466 Hwy. 29, Rutherford, 800/446-7358, www.peju.com, 10am-6pm daily, tasting $20), with its manicured gardens, koi pond, curiously shaped trees, and lofty tasting room in a tower replete with giant stained-glass window has the feel of a French country estate viewed through a hallucinogenic haze. This may reflect owner Anthony Peju's curious path to the Napa Valley from his homeland of Azerbaijan by way of France, England, and Los Angeles.

Apart from the curious trees, Peju is perhaps best known for its cabernet franc, but that's one wine that's usually not available for tasting due to its almost cultlike status. Instead, visitors can taste the equally outstanding estate cabernet sauvignon and the unusual Provence table wine, a dark rosé blend of almost all the other varietals Peju grows—merlot, cabernet franc, and syrah, plus the white colombard and sauvignon blanc. Those varietals, together with zinfandel, are also available as separate wines, many sold only through the winery. Peju is open later than most in the area, but during particularly crowded times you might find getting into the tasting room involves a bit of a wait.

◖ INGLENOOK
When a fabled Hollywood director buys one of the most storied of the historic Napa Valley wineries, it's somewhat inevitable that the result would be one of the most impressive winery shows in the valley. And so it is at **Inglenook** (1991 St. Helena Hwy., Rutherford, 707/968-1100, www.inglenook.com, 10am-5pm daily, tour and tasting $50), which was formerly Rubicon and formerly Niebaum-Coppola.

The Inglenook Estate was established in 1871 by the son-in-law of George Yount, the first white settler in Napa Valley, who is also credited with planting the first vineyard in the valley in 1838. By the 1950s Inglenook had earned a reputation as the maker of the best wines in the valley. Unfortunately, shortly thereafter, the estate was sold (including the name) piece by piece. In 1975, Francis Ford Coppola, hot on the heels of *The Godfather*, bought a part of it. Since then, he has worked hard to reunite the original estate, including the name, "Inglenook," which he bought from the conglomerate Wine Group in 2011. Today, the Inglenook is fully restored, and now a great effort is under way to re-create the style of wines made in the winery's heyday.

All this may sound like film (or wine) industry bluster, but the effort is taken very seriously. In fact, the Hollywood sheen (fountains, pergolas, etc.) on the historic, ivy-clad winery might have created a theme-park-like experience, but in reinventing Inglenook, the Coppolas have taken a different path. For example, there are no tasting rooms. To taste the wines, you must sign up (advance reservations are recommended) for a tour and tasting, or a seated tasting paired with cheese or small bites. These generally last an hour and a half and occur daily. While the price is stiff (all around $50), the tours are fascinating and the food pairings are significant enough to serve as lunch.

Another option is to simply stop by the Bistro. With indoor seating as well as tables scattered around a leafy patio, this is a European-style café with small menu of French-inspired salads and sandwiches, which pair perfectly with the wines, available by the glass and by the bottle. If you want a casual tasting at Inglenook, buying a glass (or two) at the Bistro is your only option.

GRGICH HILLS WINERY

The tasting room at **Grgich Hills Winery** (1829 St. Helena Hwy., Rutherford, 800/532-3057, www.grgich.com, daily 9:30am-4:30pm, tasting $15) isn't housed in the most elaborate building. The gardens aren't showy, and the working vineyards run right up to the back of the winemaking facility. Active aging barrels crowd the main building and narrow the path to the tasting room's restrooms. If you're looking for a showy Napa Valley "experience," this might not be the best place for you.

What you *will* find at Grgich are some of the best wines in the valley, an entirely biodynamic winemaking operation, and the rich history of fine wine from California taking its rightful place alongside and even ahead of the great French vintages. Mike Grgich took his California chardonnay to the 1976 Paris wine tasting and entered it in the white burgundy blind-tasting competition. It won. The French winemakers were incensed at the result and demanded that the contest be re-run. Grgich's chardonnay won again. (That same year, Robert Mondavi's cabernet sauvignon also took top honors in its category at the same contest.) The quality of California wines could no longer be ignored by even the snottiest of French wine connoisseurs.

Today, you'll learn about this history when visiting Grgich Hills. You'll also see plenty of information about biodynamic farming, a process that takes organic to the next level, using all-natural processes and including phenomena such as the phases of the moon in the growing and harvesting cycles of the vineyards. All Grgich wines are biodynamically grown and made. Their best wine might be the descendants of Mike's legendary chardonnay—arguably the best chardonnay made in Napa or anywhere else in California. But don't ignore

the reds; Grgich offers some lovely zinfandels and cabernets. And the Violetta, a dessert wine named for Mike's daughter, is a special treat that's only made in years when the grape conditions are perfect. None of the Grgich wines are cheap, and there's a fee for tasting, but it's more than worth it when you sip these rare, exquisite vintages.

BEAULIEU VINEYARD

A giant ivy-clad winery building that looks as dominant as any in the Napa Valley is a reminder of the huge role **Beaulieu Vineyard** (1960 St. Helena Hwy., Rutherford, 800/373-5896, www.bvwines.com, tasting and tours 10am-5pm daily, tasting $15-35) played in the modern California wine industry. Founded in 1900 by Frenchman Georges de Latour, BV now makes well over one million cases of wine per year, although the best Napa Valley wines available here represent only a fraction of the total. BV is perhaps best known for its powerful, dusty cabernet sauvignons, in particular the flagship Georges Latour Private Reserve. It also makes a full range of other red and white wines from its Napa Valley vineyards, four of which can be sampled on the red-only or white-only tasting menu ($15).

The best option, however, are the three cabernet-focused tasting options. One includes some clonal bottlings ($20), and another is the private tasting where a "wine educator" discusses the expression of *terroir* in each vintage ($25). For $35 you can enjoy a horizontal or vertical tasting of the single-vineyard reserves, including the Latour, that is offered in the impressive new reserve tasting room, which has rich stonework, subdued lighting, and a marble-topped tasting bar that does a good job of conveying the appropriate degree of gravitas for wines that helped put California on the world wine map. A tasting of some of BV's best cabernets is also part of the $40 appointment-only tour of the historic winery and its cellars. A more history-oriented tour is available for $20 that includes a barrel tasting of two cabernets. These occur at 11am and 2:30pm daily and are appointment only.

⚡ FROG'S LEAP WINERY

Unlike many of his haughty neighbors, the owner of **Frog's Leap Winery** (8815 Conn Creek Rd., Rutherford, 707/963-4704 or 800/959-4704, www.frogsleap.com, 10am-4pm daily, tasting $20), John Williams, injects some fun into the often staid Napa wine scene, from the name of the winery and its classy black-and-white deco-style wine labels to a wine called Leapfrogmilch (a blend of riesling and chardonnay, and a perfect picnic wine) and the ever-present winery motto "Time's fun when you're having flies."

Williams has also been dedicated to using organic farming practices all along, and Frog's Leap is now regarded as a champion of organic practices in the valley. It also has a big organic vegetable and fruit garden, and visitors can usually help themselves to produce, which can generally be found in a box by the main door. When driving up, the big historic red barn is the landmark to look out for, as there are precious few signs identifying the winery from the road.

Almost half of the wine made here is the excellent and well-priced sauvignon blanc, but Frog's Leap is also known for its cabernet sauvignon, zinfandel, and the flagship Rutherford, a Bordeaux-style red blend that highlights the unique fruit-meets-earth characteristics of Rutherford appellation wines. The portfolio also includes merlot, chardonnay, syrah, and a wine called (appropriately enough) Pink, which is another fun and cheap picnic wine.

No appointment is needed to visit the winery, and you can often taste the wine of the day for free. A flight of four wines occurs on the wraparound porch or inside the newly built vineyard house, accompanied by cheese, crackers, and jam. On a tour (highly recommended), you also get a tasting of four wines, but each tasting is enjoyed somewhere different along the tour, be it the garden, red barn, or the vineyard. Tours occur at 10:30am and 2:30pm daily, last about an hour, and cost the same as a tasting, but you must book them in advance.

ZD WINES

There is no doubt about it, the high-quality wines and $10 tasting fee found at **ZD Wines** (8383 Silverado Trail, Napa, 800/487-7757, www.zdwines.com, 10am-4:30pm daily, tasting $10-20) are a refreshing change from the many pricier, hit-and-miss tasting room experiences elsewhere in the valley. For the price you'll taste outstanding chardonnay and pinot from its Carneros vineyards, and the recently added rich cabernet sauvignon from other Napa appellations. Tours of the winery, including a barrel tasting, are also available by appointment for $40, but the better touring option is the $50 ecotour that takes visitors out into an organic cabernet vineyard to discuss the principles of Wine Country organic farming.

Taking pricey Napa cabernet to the extreme, ZD also makes limited quantities of its Abacus wine each year from a blend of all its previous vintages of reserve cabernet, starting from 1992. In 2010, Abacus XII was released, containing 17 former vintages. The idea is to combine the best aspects of aged wine with the fruit of more youthful wine. You'll have to pay upward of $525 per bottle to find out if it succeeds, or sign up with five other friends for a tasting ($650 for the entire group) that includes cheese, truffles, flights of some reserve wines, and a whole bottle of Abacus.

MUMM NAPA

A late starter among the French champagne houses to set up in California is **Mumm Napa** (8445 Silverado Trail, Rutherford, 800/686-6272, http://mummnapa.com, daily 10am-4:45pm, tasting $7-40). There is definitely a corporate air about the operations here, but not really more so than at many other large valley wineries, and the unassuming redwood winery building is refreshingly low-key. The wines range from the classic and reasonably priced Brut Prestige, a dry blend of pinot noir and chardonnay, up to the more fruit-forward and expensive DVX, which comes in white and rosé styles. Mumm also makes a winery-only pinot gris still wine, which is perfect for a picnic but tends to sell out quickly.

Tastings happen at tables (indoors or outside on the terrace overlooking the vineyards), with menus and service in restaurant fashion. Yes, the prices look very Napa Valley, but you'll get more wine and service for your money at Mumm. Each pour is three ounces of wine—some of it high-end—and you get three pours per tasting. Be prepared to wait on holiday weekends or at other busy times because lines often snake out the door. A seat is not essential; you can stroll over to the small art gallery, glass in hand, to see the permanent collection of about 30 original Ansel Adams prints as well as other photography exhibits that change several times a year. Large windows in the gallery give tantalizing views of the barrel and triage rooms below.

Those who prefer to learn more about what they are drinking and seeing should take the informative (and free) tour that starts promptly at 10am. While it does not include a tasting, you will receive a 15 percent-off coupon toward a bottle of bubbly. If 10am is too early, tours are available at 11am, 1pm, and 3pm, but they cost $10, or $25 with a tasting.

RUTHERFORD HILL WINERY

One of the best merlots for the price and certainly the best winery picnic grounds in the valley can be found at **Rutherford Hill Winery** (200 Rutherford Hill Rd., Rutherford, 707/963-1871, www.rutherfordhill.com, 10am-5pm daily, tasting $15-30), housed in a giant barnlike redwood building just a mile up the hill from the Silverado Trail (and neighboring the Auberge du Soleil resort). Rutherford Hill also makes small quantities of a lot of other wines that never seem to garner quite the same praise as the merlot. They include cabernet sauvignon and a couple of chardonnays, syrah, cabernet franc, and sangiovese, all from Napa Valley vineyards.

But a chilled bottle of sauvignon blanc or rosé of merlot are perhaps the best wines to grab for a picnic in one of the two oak-shaded picnic grounds, both of which offer tantalizing glimpses through the trees of the valley far below. The view also takes in the rooftops of the exclusive Auberge du Soleil resort just down the hill, so even if you can't afford to stay there, you can at least see what some of the fuss is about.

To cool off, sign up for a tour of the winery, which includes its extensive cave system. Here, more than a mile of tunnels can store about 8,000 barrels of wine and impress even jaded wine lovers. Tours are offered three times a day at 11:30am, 1:30pm, and 3:30pm for $30 and include a tasting.

RAYMOND VINEYARDS

Named 2012 American Winery of the Year by the *Wine Enthusiast*, **Raymond Vineyards** (849 Zinfandel Ln., St. Helena, 707/963-6929, www.raymondvineyards.com, 10am-4pm daily, tasting $20-30) has deep family roots in the fabled Napa Valley. Roy Raymond Sr. arrived in Napa in 1933 and worked for 35 years at Beringer Winery. But in 1970, the Raymond family decided it was time to start their own business. Raymond Vineyards earned accolades for elegant, complex, and well-balanced wines. For five generations the family worked side-by-side on every aspect of the winery business, from farming and fermentation to bottling and sales. In 2009, charismatic wine icon Jean-Charles Boisset purchased the winery as part of his Boisset Family Estates collection, which includes DeLoach Vineyards and Buena Vista. Boisset is committed to honoring the spirit and quality that Raymond Vineyards maintained, but he also imbues the winery with his own signature style of luxury and a touch of eccentricity. Boisset has created a fantasy palace for the senses—from the Crystal Cellar dripping with Baccarat chandeliers to the Corridor of Senses with its "Touch Station" to the educational outdoor Theater of Nature. Enjoy sips of expertly crafted cabernet sauvignon, chardonnay, merlot, sauvignon blanc, and some small-lot varietals while you experience this eye-popping winery.

Wineries by Appointment
CAYMUS VINEYARDS

This is a great example of how wineries on this side of the valley turn out some of the best

ORGANIC? BIODYNAMIC? WHAT'S IN A NAME?

It may be difficult to imagine that many Napa Valley wineries started in the 1970s and early 1980s began as a sort of back-to-the-land endeavor. As such, many were the first large-scale champions of organic farming, eschewing synthetic fertilizers, herbicides, and pesticides in favor of natural methods to combat weeds, pest, and disease.

Biodynamic farming takes this principle even further. Pioneered by Rudolph Steiner, the godfather of Waldorf Education, biodynamics attempts to re-create the natural interactions of all aspects of the environment. This includes promoting biodiversity on the farm, utilizing animal husbandry, planting and harvesting in concert with the moon's cycles, and using elements in the soil to boost health.

BENZIGER FAMILY WINERY

The best biodynamic tour in Wine Country is at **Benziger Family Winery** (1883 London Ranch Rd., Glen Ellen, 888/490-2739, www. benziger.com). At Benziger, the overgrown-looking vineyards are planted in cover crops such as vetch or mustard. The mountaintop winery also shelters 30 acres of woods and

wetlands, and the Insectory garden, in the middle of the vineyards, is planted with native flowers to attract dynamic pest-fighting insects. Cows and sheep mow the grasses and fertilize the land, but the more entertaining (and nonnative) peacocks had to be fenced in because they were playing havoc with the vines. Benziger, along with a handful of Mendocino wineries, was ahead of the curve, and is today one of the best examples of biodynamic farming in Wine Country.

Tours: The 45-minute tour costs $20 and is offered daily every half hour 11am-3:30pm. The tour includes a tasting, but fills up fast, especially in summer and on the weekends. Tickets are available at the winery, but booking ahead online is recommended. If you can't make a tour, take the self-guided Biodynamic Discovery Trail just off the parking lot.

CLIF FAMILY WINERY

The **Clif Family Winery** (707/968-0625, www.cliffamilywinery.com), of Clif Bar fame, is home to vegetables, fruit trees, olive trees, chickens, turkeys, and honey bees. Visitors can learn how these elements work together in a

wines with little fanfare. The Caymus family has been farming in the valley for more than 100 years but was ahead of the modern wine rush when they ripped up their prune orchards to plant vines in the early 1970s.

Since then, **Caymus Vineyards** (8700 Conn Creek Rd., Rutherford, 707/967-3010, www. caymus.com, by appointment 10am-4pm daily, tasting $30) gained a reputation for producing one of the best Napa cabernets, the Special Selection, made with the best grapes from the estate vineyard in Rutherford. It garners regular praise from all the major critics and is usually on the tasting flight at the sit-down, appointment-only tasting. The other well-known Caymus wine is a nonreserve cabernet

that is equally impressive and half the price. A less well-known wine, but one to look out for nonetheless, is the outstanding zinfandel that is sold only at the winery.

Don't come expecting a flashy Napa-style spectacle for the money. This is definitely a winery tasting experience for those serious about their wines, but gardening aficionados will also get a kick from the pretty surroundings.

CHILES VALLEY WINERIES

The Chiles Valley is easy to reach. Take Highway 128 (Sage Canyon Road) up into the hills from the Silverado Trail at Rutherford, past Lake Hennessey, and go sustainable way, and are treated afterward to a tasting at the winery's St. Helena tasting room, **Velo Vino** (709 Main St., St. Helena).

Tours: Appointment-only tours cost $80 and are offered at 10am daily May-October (48-hours advance reservation required).

FROG'S LEAP

John Williams at **Frog's Leap** (8815 Conn Creek Rd., Rutherford, 707/963-4704 or 800/959-4704, www.frogsleap.com) was the first in the valley to certify his vineyards organic in 1988. Williams does not use any synthetic inputs (fertilizers, herbicides, and pesticides) to combat weeds, pests, and disease or to boost the fertility of the soil. Instead, he relies upon "organic" or naturally occurring methods like cover crops and mechanical weed control to keep his vines healthy. In keeping with its green credentials, Frog's Leap is also certified biodynamic under the international Demeter certification organization. Take a tour to learn about Williams's approach to sustainability (solar power, a geo-thermal heating and cooling system, LEED-certified buildings, and farming without irrigation).

Tours: Tours are Monday-Friday at 10:30am

and 2:30pm. The $20 fee includes a tasting of four current-release wines.

LONG MEADOW RANCH

Perhaps the king of Napa Valley farm tours is **Long Meadow Ranch** (738 Main St., St. Helena, 707/963-4555, www.longmeadowranch.com). Sustainable farming is the byword here, as the huge piles of compost suggest. Grass-fed beef, eggs, vegetables, and fruit are all part of the organic bounty. Even the winery building is a model of sustainable practices: The walls are made from compressed earth dug out during construction of the caves, and all power is provided by solar panels. On the appointment-only tour, a vintage Swiss Pinzgauer ferries visitors up narrow mountain roads to the 650-acre ranch and winery. During the tour, the principles of grape and olive growing and organic farming practices are explained. After returning to the winery building, a three-course meal is the culmination of the tour.

Tours: Book tours at least two days in advance. The early tour starts at 10:30am (includes lunch) and costs $195. The afternoon tour leaves at 3:30pm (includes dinner) and costs $225.

either left or right at the junction. Both roads lead to the valley. Just be sure to leave plenty of time to drive there and back on the mountain roads and to take lunch, because there's very little apart from farmland and vineyards up there.

Wineries by Appointment
RUSTRIDGE RANCH & WINERY

About three miles from Lake Hennessey on Chiles Pope Valley Road, turn right onto Lower Chiles Valley Road to get to this very rustic part-winery, part-ranch, where thoroughbred horses are just as important as wine. Tastings at **RustRidge** (2910 Lower Chiles Valley Rd., St. Helena, 707/965-9353, www.rustridge.com, by

appointment 10am-4pm daily, tasting $20-50) are held in an old cattle barn that now houses the winery workings, and a visit here is as much about smelling the horses as the wine.

About 55 of the ranch's 440 acres are planted with grapes, and the winery makes about 2,000 cases of zinfandel, both barrel- and tank-fermented chardonnay, cabernet sauvignon, and sauvignon blanc. There are daily tastings at 11am, 1pm, or 3pm, and you must call ahead to reserve a spot. Once seated, you'll taste five or six estate wines. There is also a reserve tasting for $40, a chocolate pairing for $30, and a food pairing for $50. Afterward, guests are encouraged to picnic, visit the horses, and enjoy the scenery.

KULETO ESTATE

When one of the Bay Area's most successful restaurateurs turns his hand to winemaking, you can be sure the resulting winery is going to be quite a destination. The **Kuleto Estate** winery (2470 Sage Canyon Rd., St. Helena, 707/302-2200, www.kuletoestate.com, tours by appointment 10:30am, 11:45am, 1pm, and 2:30pm daily, $40) does not disappoint, from the secret gate code given to visitors who make an appointment to the Tuscan-style house, Villa Cucina, with its infinity pool framing a view of Lake Hennessey and the valley beyond.

Pat Kuleto is the man behind such swank San Francisco restaurants as Boulevard and Farallon. On his expansive Napa estate, 800 acres of former grazing land, he has planted 90 acres of vineyards, predominantly cabernet sauvignon and sangiovese, with small blocks of zinfandel, syrah, pinot noir, and chardonnay. Such variety leads to a diverse portfolio of estate wines. Tours of the diverse vineyards and modern winery, together with a comprehensive tasting of wines, are available four times a day by appointment.

RECREATION

If you're looking for a lake vacation adjacent to Wine Country, drive a few miles out to **Lake Berryessa** (Berryessa-Knoxville Rd., east of Rutherford). On this largish lake you can ride powerboats, Jet Ski, kayak, canoe, and fish— or just sunbathe on the shore and splash about in the shallows with your family. If you've got your own boat, you can launch it at one of the marinas or the **Capell Cove Boat Ramp** (Knoxville Rd.). Or you can rent from one of the lakeside resorts. The **Markley Cove Resort** (7521 Hwy. 128, Napa, 707/966-4204, www.lakeberryessaboats.com) offers all kinds of boats, from patio cruisers to high-end ski-tow boats to personal watercraft to kayaks. Make reservations well in advance to get the boat you want! You can also rent water skis, wakeboards, and ski tubes.

Lake Berryessa also boasts some of the best fishing in California. You can fish for cold- and warm-water fish, including bass, rainbow trout, and kokanee salmon. Rent a boat from one of the resorts, launch your own, or enjoy some relaxed fishing from the shore. The resorts can sell California fishing licenses and bait, and advise you about the season's hottest fishing holes.

ACCOMMODATIONS

High up in the eastern hills of the valley, bathed in afternoon sun and buzzing with the sound of the golf carts used to ferry guests around, is ◖ **Auberge du Soleil** (180 Rutherford Hill Rd., Rutherford, 707/963-1211 or 800/348-5406, www.aubergedusoleil.com, $700), or the Inn of the Sun, one of the valley's most luxurious resorts, famous for being the hangout of the rich, the famous, and lucky honeymooners. This is a place totally at ease with itself, where the decor plays a relaxed second fiddle to the stunning location rather than competing with it. Terra-cotta tiles, natural woods, fireplaces, leather, and earth tones hint at some French country style, but it's the views from almost everywhere that dominate. Work out in the gym with views, eat with views at the acclaimed restaurant, swim with views, or step out of your room's French doors onto a balcony with views. Just be prepared to pay dearly for those views, the amenities, and the exclusivity of the whole place. Whether they're worth the money is open to debate, but Auberge regularly shows up on lists of the world's top hotels, and its rates have climbed significantly in recent years, suggesting there is no shortage of people willing to empty their bank accounts for the privilege of staying here.

There are 50 rooms and suites in cottages spread throughout the 33 lush acres of this former olive grove, and all have the word *view* in their descriptions. The cheapest and smallest are the Hilltop View rooms in the main building upstairs from the restaurant and bar, though they "may be inappropriate for light sleepers," the resort suggests. Slightly larger rooms are in better locations, and the mammoth suites are the size of a typical apartment, and cost about the same per night as rent would for the month.

A bit more down-to-earth than Auberge in

terms of price, altitude, and attitude is the cozy **Rancho Caymus Inn** (1140 Rutherford Rd., Rutherford, 707/963-1777 or 800/845-1777, www.ranchocaymus.com, $180-389). Wood beams and floors, adobe walls, and quirky design elements, including hand-dyed South American rugs and carved headboards, give this 26-room Spanish-style inn a rustic hand-crafted charm. Modern amenities are some-what lacking, but the rooms all have private bathrooms, small patios overlooking the lush gardens, wet bars and refrigerators, and a sepa-rate seating area that make them more like ju-nior suites. All but the smallest Caymus Suites have fireplaces. Some of the more expensive suites also have whirlpool tubs.

FOOD

If a special occasion requires a special restau-rant (and French Laundry is not answering the phone), there's probably no better place in this part of the valley than **Auberge du Soleil** (180 Rutherford Hill Rd., 800/348-5406, reserva-tions required, 7am-11am, 11:30am-2:30pm, and 5:30pm-9:30pm daily, tasting menu $150). You don't need to be a guest to see why this resort restaurant has been wowing diners with its menu and stunning views of the valley since 1981. The wow factor is still as strong as ever and might make you want to stay at the resort on your next visit (after saving up, that is).

The exquisitely prepared French-Californian food is not as expensive as you'd think—the $150 set price buys you a four-course dinner with plenty of choices for every course (al-though that doesn't include wine, of course). Just make sure you choose a fine day, and try to get a table out on the terrace for the views, especially at sunset. And casual as it might be, this is still a fancy restaurant, so don't turn up in baggy shorts and flip-flops. If you're not ready to commit to such an indul-gent affair, consider visiting the adjacent **Bistro & Bar** (11am-11pm daily, $20). You can choose from braised short ribs, a plate of charcuterie, or a light salad to accompany the rotating and wide selection of wines. You can still take in the luxurious atmosphere (wraparound deck,

open fireplace) without quite the pinch to your belt or wallet.

For some more down-to-earth dining, often without the need for a reservation, the **Rutherford Grill** (1180 Rutherford Rd., Rutherford, 707/963-1792, 11:30am-9:30pm Sun.-Thurs., 11:30am-10:30pm Fri.-Sat., dinner entrées $15-40) offers traditional steak house fare in a slightly corporate setting that hints at the fact that it is owned by the Houston's res-taurant chain. Nevertheless, it has become one of the most popular steak houses among Napa Valley residents and is a great place for a reliably cooked and aged steak to pair with a well-aged Rutherford cabernet. This is not the place to go for cutting-edge California cuisine, but it is the place for a classic steak dinner. There's also a nice shady patio, although it's a little too close to the road to be classified as peaceful.

Picnic Supplies

For a picnic lunch, or just a few munchies for the road, stop by the **Oakville Grocery** (7856 St. Helena Hwy., Oakville, 707/944-8802, www.oakvillegrocery.com, 7am-5pm Mon.-Thurs., 7am-6pm Fri.-Sat., 8am-5pm Sun., $10). A long-standing Napa Valley institution, the Oakville Grocery's reputation for stocking only the best food, wine, cheese, and other goodies make it a must-stop for many traveling up Highway 29. Browse the tightly packed shelves or order a hot lunch at the center counter. This historic grocery, opened in 1881, has been recently re-vamped and has everything from crab cakes to chimichangas to boxed lunches. Look out for the large *Coca-Cola* sign painted on the south side of the building. It will help, if you are traveling north, at least, to not miss the quick turnout.

INFORMATION AND SERVICES

Oakville and Rutherford are the only districts along Highway 29 without a visitors center or even a center of town. For more information on the area, visit the **visitors centers** in St. Helena (657 Main St., 707/963-4456, www.sthelena.com, 9am-5pm Mon.-Fri., 10am-5pm Sat.-Sun.) or Yountville (6484 Washington St.,

707/944-0904, http://yountville.com, 10am–5pm daily). The people behind the desk will likely have the answers to your questions plus various coupons for tasting at Oakville and Rutherford wineries. You will also find plenty of information at any tasting room you visit and local institutions like the Oakville Grocery. Don't expect much in the way of free Wi-Fi, but cell reception is generally reliable here. Any banking needs should be done in Napa or St. Helena.

GETTING THERE AND AROUND

A few miles north of Yountville, on Highway 29, you'll find Oakville and Rutherford, but their loose organization and rural character may cause you to miss them if you are not alert. You can reach the Silverado Trail on Oakville Road in Oakville and by Rutherford Road (also Highway 128) in Rutherford. The Oakville Grade is one of the few roads on Highway 29 that crosses the Mayacamus Mountains into the neighboring Sonoma Valley, connecting with Highway 12 in Glen Ellen after over 10 twisty miles.

The area is relatively easy to navigate, as there are few streets interrupting the acres of vineyards. However, street signs can be difficult to see, especially while watching out for tipsy drivers.

St. Helena and Vicinity

St. Helena has been the center of the valley's wine industry from the very beginning. George Crane first planted grapes in the area in 1861, followed by Charles Krug a few years later. With the new wine industry springing up all around, the town grew rapidly and was incorporated in 1876, only a few years after Napa and many years before Calistoga in 1885.

St. Helena's history has been inextricably linked to the valley's wine industry ever since. Calistoga to the north had its spas to draw visitors, and Napa to the south became a thriving commercial port city, gateway to the valley, but to a certain extent St. Helena has always been a tourist town. Wealthy weekenders came here to wine and dine in the early 1900s, an influx of European immigrants created the thriving Italian and French heritage, and the town was the epicenter of the valley's bootlegging industry during Prohibition, making the St. Helena Highway (Highway 29, to locals) almost as busy in the 1930s as it is today.

St. Helena has often been derided as the town that sold its soul to tourism, but don't be fooled into thinking that it is resting on its Victorian charm. Behind the historic 19th-century storefront facades sits an amazing collection of modern art. Recently, a sophisticated set of serious art lovers have moved into town, opening galleries, "showrooms," and, of course, tasting rooms. Edgy and compelling, these spaces show internationally acclaimed artists, rivaling their big-city counterparts for relevance in the modern art world.

The Wines

As the Napa Valley gets narrower farther north and the mountains ever more sheltering, the weather gets hotter. The **St. Helena** appellation includes the narrowest point of the valley and also some of the biggest and most historic winery names, like Beringer, Charles Krug, and Louis Martini. The heat and rich alluvial soils are responsible for wines that help give the Napa Valley its name for rich and highly extracted wines. You'll know a St. Helena cabernet when you taste one—big, bold, and powerful.

West of St. Helena, up the slopes of the Mayacamas Mountains, is the **Spring Mountain** appellation, an area with almost as much winemaking history as the valley floor below. The region gets its name from the many springs and creeks—there's actually not a peak called Spring Mountain. The mountain wineries here make cabernet sauvignon and merlot with uncommon density and power. White wines are less common but include sauvignon blanc with a classic mountain minerality. As with many mountain-grown wines, however, the reds can be less approachable when young than those from the valley floor, but they tend to be more consistent year to year and usually only need a few years of aging to reach their full potential.

ST. HELENA WINERIES
V. SATTUI WINERY
To say this place gets crowded in the summer is like saying the Napa Valley is an undiscovered wine region. **V. Sattui Winery** (1111 White Ln., St. Helena, 707/963-7774, www.vsattui. com, 9am-5pm daily, tasting $10) has become a victim of its own success, and can resemble a supermarket the night before Thanksgiving as hordes descend on the pretty winery for its extensive deli and even more extensive list of well-priced wines. This is picnic central (and often party central) in this part of the valley, though after eating enough free deli samples, you might not need to buy picnic supplies. The pungent smell of the dozens of cheeses and countless other gourmet foods fills the tasting room of the stone winery building, while on summer tasted for a modest weekends hardly an inch of grass is visible outside in the two-acre picnic area as tour buses disgorge their stumbling passengers.

The reason for its popularity is simple—this is the only place in the valley where you can buy good food and cheap wines, then plop yourself down on the grass right outside to eat and drink. You just have to ignore the constant drone of traffic from the main road and the shrieks of drunken visitors.

V. Sattui now makes about 45,000 cases of wine each year, with many bottles costing less than $20, and has won several "Winery of the Year" awards from the State Fair. You will not find any reviews from magazine critics, however, because Sattui wines cannot be bought at any wine shop. The entire production is sold at the winery and through the Sattui wine clubs, making this one of the most successful

direct-to-consumer wineries in California. The huge portfolio includes a host of great picnic wines, like the popular Gamay Rouge rosé (both still and sparkling forms), a dry riesling, and a tangy sangiovese. Cabernet sauvignon in both blended and vineyard-designate styles is what the winery is perhaps best known for. All can be tasted for a modest $10 (which also adds to the popularity), but despite the multiple tasting bars you might have to wait awhile for space to open up.

Also worth trying are the dessert wines, including delicious madeira and juicy muscat. Buy a case of any wine and you instantly become a member of the Cellar Club, which has its own tasting bar.

HEITZ
One of the oldest wineries in the valley, **Heitz** (436 St. Helena Hwy., St. Helena, 707/963-3542, www.heitzcellar.com, 11am-4:30pm daily, free tasting) brings a touch of class to the glitz and glamour of Napa. The elegant, high-ceilinged tasting room is dominated by a stone fireplace with comfy chairs before it. (Be sure to say hello to Ruby, the small pampered dog rescued a couple of years ago by the winery staff.) A low bar off to the right sets the stage for an array of Napa Valley cabernet sauvignons. To the happy surprise of many, Heitz's cabernets are well balanced and easy to drink, and though costly, they approach affordable by Napa standards. Most of the grapes in these wines grow right in the Napa Valley. If you're lucky enough to visit Heitz in February, you can taste the current release of the Martha's Vineyard cabernet—a vintage grown in the first wine-designated vineyard (i.e., the first vineyard to grow grapes for wine rather than eating) in all of Napa.

HALL
When you visit **Hall** winery (401 St. Helena Hwy. S., St. Helena, 707/967-2626 or 866/667-4255, www.hallwines.com, 10am-5:30pm daily, tasting $20) you will notice two things. One is that the Halls are big fans of modern art and design; the other is that their winery

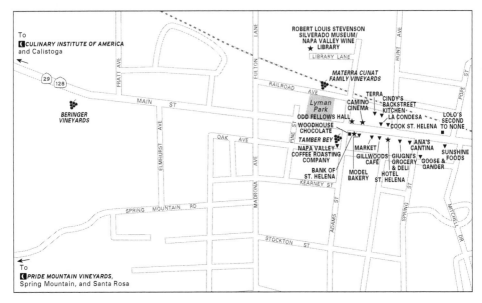

is the first LEED-Gold certified winery in California, a fact of which they are very proud. You may also notice that Hall is going through a big face-lift. Currently one of the largest land-owners in the valley, Hall is in the process of rebuilding its visitors center. As of this printing, the new visitors center is due to open September 2013. It will sit on two acres and feature a full garden.

Until then, the relaxed tasting room is in what looks like a shabby-chic cottage-style building with a large shaded patio. But as you approach the entrance with its bright red awning, don't be fooled by the peeling paint on the exterior—it was hand-painted to look shabby-chic and is just another artistic addition to the many sculptures on the grounds from the Halls' private collection. Behind it is the former Napa Valley Cooperative Winery, a warehouse-like facility built around an old stone winery dating from 1885. The original winery is an important piece of valley history that will be uncovered and form the centerpiece of the new winery complex.

The Halls have another winery, the exclusive **Hall-Rutherford,** in the hills above Auberge du Soleil across the valley, which is open to the public by appointment only and is where a high-end cabernet sauvignon is made from the Sacrashe estate vineyard. Tours are a pricey $40, but the centerpiece of the caves, a spectacular sculpture/chandelier of a grapevine root, might be, depending on your love of modern art, worth it. If not, you might be lucky enough to taste this wine, along with more reasonably priced Hall wines, including cabernet sauvignon, merlot, and sauvignon blanc.

LOUIS M. MARTINI WINERY
The hulking winery of **Louis M. Martini** (254 St. Helena Hwy., St. Helena, 707/968-3362, www.louismartini.com, 10am-6pm daily, tasting $15-30) is the place to come for cabernet lovers. The 300,000 cases of wine made here each year are dominated by various iterations of cabernet sauvignon, from appellation-specific bottlings to vineyard-specific and right down to lot-specific. The few other non-cabernet wines on the list include a petite sirah and meritage blend that is arguably a better value and more approachable than some of the cabs. Many of the best wines come from the Monte

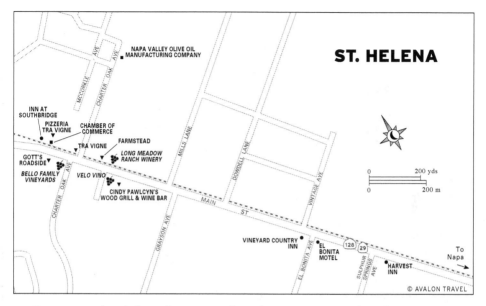

Rosso vineyard, including cabernets, a zinfandel, and a syrah. For the price of a tasting, you get a flight of three wines. You can select from the $15, $20, or $30 tastings, and, as you would expect, the most prestigious wines go with the priciest tasting, but all the wines available are noteworthy, if not award winning. A sheltered patio has tables and chairs for those who want to linger, and Martini is open at least half an hour later than most neighboring wineries, making it a good last stop.

BERINGER VINEYARDS
The oldest continuously operated winery in Napa Valley is now a huge tourist attraction that often contributes to St. Helena's summer traffic jams, though it is still worth a visit (ideally midweek, when it's a bit quieter) for its significance in the valley's wine history and for some outstanding reserve wines.

Beringer Vineyards (2000 Main St., St. Helena, 707/963-7115, www.beringer.com, 10am-6pm daily June-Oct., 10am-5pm daily Nov.-May, tasting $20-25) was established in 1876. The winery operated through Prohibition. Beringer is one of a handful of

historic wineries in the valley (others include Inglenook, Beaulieu, and Larkmead) credited with helping modernize the wine industry after Prohibition by introducing European-style production techniques and quality control rather than making cheap bulk wines. The entire estate, including the lavish and ornate Rhine House built by Frederick Beringer to remind him of home, was placed on the National Register of Historic Places in 2001.

Beautifully maintained, the Rhine House is an impressive location to taste some of Beringer's best wines, most notably its Private Reserve chardonnay and cabernet sauvignon, which are both beloved by well-known U.S. wine critics.

For $25 you may sample three wines from the reserve list in the main house. You can also make an appointment for a more civilized and relaxing reserve tasting on the porch of the Rhine House surrounded by greenery for the same price. The regular tasting in the old winery building up the hill costs just $20 for one of several themed flights of wine, but the atmosphere is far less enjoyable than the wood-paneled and stained-glass charm of the Rhine

© ELIZABETH LINHART VENEMAN

the Rhine House at Beringer Vineyards

House unless you draw a particularly entertaining and generous pourer.

The half-hour-long tours at Beringer are also well worth experiencing, offering plenty of wine education, history, and a tasting for not much more than a tasting alone would cost. They are generally offered eight times a day; check the website for exact times. For $40 you can opt for the Taste of Beringer Tour, which has a winemaking focus and takes in vineyards, the 19th-century hand-dug caves, and a seated tasting paired with small bites. Reservations are strongly recommended, particularly in the summer, but you might be able to buy tickets on the same day during quieter times of the year.

The popularity of the winery along with the ticket booths adjacent to the parking lot tend to make the place feel more like a wine theme park in the summer, but the grounds are expansive enough that you can escape the worst of the crowds and take a self-guided stroll around the Rhine House and gardens to get a sense of how grand the estate must have been in its heyday.

In the summer you might also be able to help yourself to the succulent fruit from the numerous peach trees growing near the parking lot.

CHARLES KRUG WINERY

It's probably fitting that the winery founded by the grandfather of the Napa Valley wine industry, Charles Krug, was also the winery that helped start the modern-day wine dynasty of the Mondavis. Krug arrived in California in the heady days after the gold rush and fell in with the likes of Agoston Haraszthy, credited with being the first serious winemaker in the state; George Yount, father of Yountville; and Edward Bale, who built the nearby Bale Grist Mill. Krug opened his winery in 1861. In 1943 the Krug winery was purchased by Cesare Mondavi, who built a new family wine business around it, creating one of the leading wineries in the valley. After his death in 1959, however, there was a bitter feud between his two sons, Robert and Peter, that resulted in Robert establishing his own separate winery (which has since become an empire), while Peter's side of the family held on to and still controls the Charles Krug business.

With a history like that, it's hardly surprising that parts of the **Charles Krug Winery** (2800 Main St., St. Helena, 707/967-2200 or 800/682-5784, www.charleskrug.com, 10:30am-5pm daily, tasting $15-25) are historic landmarks, including the stately old Carriage House and giant redwood cellar building. Tours were curtailed in 2007 in order to renovate some of the earthquake-unsafe buildings, but the promised reopening has yet to materialize as of early 2013. At some point the tasting room will move to the restored winery, but until then the experience of visiting a winery so steeped in history can be a little anticlimactic because the tasting room is in a small cottage standing in the shadows of the historic structures and ancient trees. That cottage has a bit of history itself, however. It is said to have been the first dedicated tasting room in the valley when it was built in the 1950s. Once inside, the wines rather than the surroundings are very much the focus.

The winery produces about 80,000 cases of wine, including just about every major varietal but specializing in cabernet sauvignon. The wines have never achieved the critical acclaim of those from the other Mondavi-related winery farther south, but recent replanting in the vineyards should eventually pay dividends. Krug does produce a handful of approachable and well-priced wines, however, including a sauvignon blanc, a Carneros pinot noir, and one of the better-value Napa Valley cabernets you'll find in this area. Hard-core cabernet lovers should focus on the reserve tasting, however, which includes some of the vineyard-specific and small-lot wines.

ST. CLEMENT VINEYARDS

After passing the big boys of Napa wine like V. Sattui, Beringer, and Krug, it's hard not to miss the quaint turreted Victorian house perched on the side of the hill west of the main road. That is **St. Clement** (2867 St. Helena Hwy. N., St. Helena, 866/877-5939, www.stclement.com, 10am-5pm Wed.-Mon., tasting $10-25), a small winery that is perhaps the prettiest in this part of the valley.

Not surprisingly, there is a variety of cabernet sauvignon from different appellations in the valley, and also the flagship Orropas red meritage blend (a backward spelling of Sapporo, the Japanese company that owned the winery until 1999). These may be tasted from the Reserve or Discovery tasting menus, or you can opt for an all-white tasting, a surprise in this part of the valley.

But wine is not the only reason to visit. St. Clement's elegant two-story Victorian farmhouse is beautifully surrounded by sloping vineyards, lush English gardens, and heavy-limbed oaks. The large split-level deck in front of the house is dotted with tables, affording both privacy and a splendid place for a picnic. (You can also make a reservation for a reserve tasting out there.) While the two tasting rooms inside can get crowded, the interior is painted deep blue with streamlined modern touches like the unique art deco chandeliers. The juxtaposition between modern and quaint is unexpected, but it works.

FREEMARK ABBEY

Despite the name, there is no religious connection with the weathered stone barn sandwiched between a brewpub and an unremarkable group of small office buildings. **Freemark Abbey** (3022 St. Helena Hwy. N., St. Helena, 800/963-9698, www.freemarkabbey.com, 10am-5pm daily, tasting $20-30) instead got its current identity in the 1940s from the nickname of Albert "Abbey" Ahern and the names of partners Charles Freeman ("Free") and Markquand Foster ("Mark"), who bought the former Lombarda Winery and its stone building, which date from 1899.

Today, Freemark Abbey is probably best known for its cabernet sauvignon, from the generic Napa Valley version to a couple of vineyard-designates, including the flagship from the Bosche Vineyard near Rutherford.

Plenty of other wines are available to try in one of the more relaxing and spacious tasting rooms in the valley, though it's in the decidedly unhistoric building next to the winery. The portfolio includes merlot, petit syrah, chardonnay, sauvignon blanc, and viognier, which may or may not be on the five-wine-tasting menu.

DUCKHORN VINEYARDS

Adjacent to Freemark Abbey is Lodi Lane, which cuts across the valley to the Silverado Trail and the impressive farmhouse-style home of **Duckhorn Vineyards** (1000 Lodi Ln. at Silverado Trail, St. Helena, 888/354-8885, www.duckhorn.com, 10am-4pm daily, tasting $30, reservations encouraged), a winery known for some outstanding merlot and cabernet sauvignon. Sauvignon blanc and semillon are the only white wines in the portfolio. Duckhorn also makes about 10,000 cases of its Paraduxx wine, a proprietary blend of zinfandel, cabernet, and merlot.

The stylish entrance lounge of the winery and the big circular tasting bar beyond, surrounded by neatly arranged tables and chairs, resemble an upscale club or restaurant, so it's no surprise that trying the wines can be pricey. But the personal service, quality wines, and peaceful veranda overlooking the vineyards make the tasting experience far more relaxing and fulfilling than at some other wineries.

Although you can visit the winery whenever you want, reservations for tastings are "strongly encouraged." During the week it's usually possible to get on the list right away, but for weekends it's best to call ahead. The flight of five wines in the basic tasting includes both Napa Valley-designated wines, while the more expensive Elevated tasting includes a tour of the winery for an extra $20. For another $30, you and a friend may pair your flights with artisan bites.

DOWNTOWN TASTING ROOMS

It used to be that visiting this picturesque Napa Valley town was a two-part proposition, or headache, as the case may be. First you had to brave traffic crawling from one winery to another on the congested Highway 29, *then* find parking downtown to enjoy its shops, restaurants, and historical atmosphere. But now the tasting rooms have arrived. At the south end of town, **Long Meadow Ranch Winery** (738 Main St., St. Helena, 707/963-4555, www.longmeadowranch.com, 11am-6pm daily, tasting $10-20) pours flights of highly regarded sauvignon blanc and cabernet sauvignon. Down the road, **Flora Springs** (677 St. Helena Hwy., St. Helena, 707/967-8032, www.florasprings.com, 10am-5pm daily, tasting $20) and **Bello Family Vineyards** (929 Main St., St. Helena, 707/967-8833, www.bellofamilyvineyards.com, 10am-5pm daily, tasting $20) are both known for their cabernet and questionable taste. It is not unusual to hear locals grumble about the tasting rooms' Orange County aesthetic. On the other hand, Orin Swift, maker of cultlike wines with provocative labels, is (as of this printing) slated to open a tasting room in May 2013 at 1325 Main Street, and is generating genuine excitement downtown. So, while some locals may complain, the new tasting rooms mean that wine lovers can taste *and* window shop without getting in the car once.

A great place to start is **Velo Vino** (709 Main St., St. Helena, 707/968-0625, www.cliffamilywinery.com, 10am-6pm daily, tasting $15), the tasting room for Clif Family Winery. If the name rings a bell, you'll place it when you enter the stand-alone tasting room where just as much space is devoted to cycling as to wine, and energy bars line the walls. Yes, this is the enological endeavor of the man behind Clif Bar. Gary Erikson and his wife, Kit, moved to the Napa Valley in 1999 and have given valley living the sort of gusto you would expect from a physical fitness enthusiast. In that short time, they started an organic farm that locals may join as a CSA member and get a box of weekly produce in the summer (farm tours are available); began bottling their own olive oil; developed a Wine Country snack food line that includes fruit preserves, spice blends, nut mixes, and mustards; and, of course, began making wine. And the wine is good, too.

Like many small wineries, Clif Family wines are not available outside their wine club or their tasting room. This is reason number one to visit. Reason number two? It is a fun tasting room. Arranged like a café, there are tables for privacy and an outdoor patio. But the best part is the bar itself. There, you are likely to see locals come in for a glass of wine ($7 white, $10 red) and horse around with the staff.

For the price of the basic tasting ($15) you can select four of the current releases, which generally include a riesling, gewürztraminer, grenache, zinfandel, and a cabernet. The Climber Limited Release is a Bordeaux-style blend, and it is exceptional, while Kit's Killer Cab has scored above 90 points with *Wine Spectator*. For an extra $10 you can nibble on Gary & Kit's Napa Valley olive oil and snacks. Cheese plates are available for $20, and for $40 you can indulge in it all at a private tasting of some of the reserve wines. Pours are generous and the atmosphere so friendly, you may not want to leave. But if you must, there is an espresso machine behind the counter to get you going. And, oh yeah, you can rent bikes here, too.

Bruce Regalia, who makes the wines for Velo Vino, is also the winemaker at **Materra Cunat Family Vineyards** (1426 Main St., St. Helena, 707/244-4600, www.materrawines. com, 11:30am-5pm Wed.-Sun., tasting $10). On the ground floor of the Wydown Hotel, the space is clearly Victorian but has been designed with a modern touch, enhanced by the cool modern art "installations" created by the youngest Cunat, Amie, a New York artist who also designed the winery's lovely labels. To taste, you're likely to be served by her older sister Neena, who is an unaffected and congenial host. For $10 you'll get three tastes. The winery makes mostly cabernet sauvignon and merlot, but the real standout (and steal at $20) is the chardonnay. The vineyard is located in the Oak Knoll appellation from which hailed the Grgich chardonnay that stole the show in Paris in 1976. Plans are in the works for a full-fledged winery and tasting room(s) at the vineyard.

Nearby on Adams Street **Tamber Bey** (1234 Adams St., St. Helena, 707/968-5345, www. tamberbey.com, 11am-8pm daily, tasting $15-25) pours sauvignon blanc, chardonnay, merlot, cabernet sauvignon, and a Bordeaux blend.

Many of the wines hail from their Oakville vineyard, also home to their stable of racing horses. The tasting room is small with a copper bar and seating that looks over the quiet street outside. Guest can enjoy a flight of three or five wines paired with savory cookies as well as half ($3-8) or full ($6-16) glasses of wine. This is not a bad option, especially as Tamber Bey is open late, making it a lovely place to conclude a long day of tasting, shopping, and eating.

Wineries by Appointment

CORISON

A rarity in the ritzy Napa Valley, **Corison** (987 St. Helena Hwy., St. Helena, 707/963-0826, www.corison.com, 10am-5pm daily, tasting $20) is the genuine article—a tiny single-proprietor winery producing great wines in small quantities. Technically, Corison takes tasters by appointment only, but in truth they've never turned away a drop-in during their regular business hours. After turning onto a short gravel driveway, you'll pass a vintage home to reach the small barn that serves as a tasting room. Open the huge white door (it's easier than it looks) and enter the tasting/barrel/stock room. A tiny bar sits right next to the entrance, offering tastings from the 3,000 cases the winery produces each year. Expect the attentive staff to talk in loving and knowledgeable terms about the delicious wines they're pouring. Corison's flagship cabernet sauvignon tastes of luscious fruit and perfect balance. The other wines are not distributed—you must buy them then and there, join the wine club, or long for them from afar.

PRAGER WINERY & PORT WORKS

Right opposite the entrance to the Louis M. Martini Winery is the little wooden sign and driveway leading to **Prager Winery** (1281 Lewelling Ln., St. Helena, 707/963-7678 or 800/969-7678, www.pragerport.com, 10am-4:30pm daily, tasting $20), a funky, family-owned port producer that is a refreshing change from the commercial atmosphere of most wineries in the area. The closest you'll find to a winery museum here is the Web Window, a masterpiece of spiderweb engineering that's supposedly been untouched since 1979.

The Prager family makes a few regular wines here (a couple are usually included in the tasting), but most of the 3,500-case annual production is an unusual selection of ports and late-harvest dessert wines, including a fruity white port made from chardonnay and the more usual vintage and tawny ports made predominantly with cabernet sauvignon and petite sirah grapes. Bring a cigar to enjoy with port out in the garden.

EHLERS ESTATE

Moderate wine consumption might be good for the heart, according to some researchers. Moderate consumption of Ehlers Estate wines is most certainly good for hearts in general. Established in 1886, the historic stone **Ehlers Estate** winery (3222 Ehlers Ln., St. Helena, 707/963-5972, www.ehlersestate.com, 10:30am-4:30pm daily by appointment, tasting $25), just north of St. Helena, is owned by the Leducq Foundation, a French charity that funds cardiovascular research at high-profile medical schools around the world including Harvard, Columbia, and the University of California at San Diego. Visiting such a nonprofit enterprise is a refreshing idea in a valley known more for unashamed hedonism.

Unlike many valley wineries, Ehlers Estate makes only estate wines from the surrounding organic and biodynamic vineyards, many of which have been replanted over the past decade. For the price of the tasting, you'll get a flight of their sauvignon blanc, cabernet franc rosé, merlot, and two cabernet sauvignons. Double the price and you can add handcrafted chocolates paired with different estate Bordeaux wines, and a tour and barrel tasting. This adventure starts at 11am

BENESSERE VINEYARDS

The family that established **Benessere Vineyards** (1010 Big Tree Rd., St. Helena, 707/963-5853, www.benesserevineyards.com, 10am-5pm daily, tasting $15-20) in 1994 does not publicize the fact that the winery used to be owned by Charles Shaw, a name that will forever be associated with the Two-Buck Chuck phenomenon of cheap and cheerful wines. Shaw owned the winery from the early 1970s but eventually sold it to the Central Valley Bronco Wine Company, which now churns out those cheap wines. The winery property itself and 42 acres of neglected vineyards were eventually bought by John and Ellen Benish in the early 1990s.

They have since transformed it into a producer of increasingly well-regarded Italian varietal wines, with the help of some expert Italian winemaking consultants. The lively and light Italian wines here are a nice diversion from the more intense cabernet and chardonnay that dominate the scene in this part of the Napa Valley, and the winery itself is at the end of a small road far off the beaten path of the St. Helena Highway (Highway 29), surrounded by aromatic gardens and guarded by a hefty Newfoundland dog. An appointment for tasting is technically necessary, but calling ahead by even an hour is usually fine during the week.

SPRING MOUNTAIN WINERIES

Exploring this lesser-known appellation makes an interesting diversion from St. Helena and is a beautiful drive. From Highway 29, turn onto Madrona Road, and Spring Mountain Road is three blocks farther on the right. Alternatively, just south of Beringer Vineyards, Elmhurst Road also leads to Spring Mountain Road. From there the road follows a creek as it climbs steeply through redwoods and oak trees, past terraced mountain vineyards and orchards, to the many small wineries that often have stunning views of the valley far below.

If you're on a schedule, be sure to leave plenty of time to visit these Spring Mountain wineries; the drive is slow and quickly becomes frustrating (and potentially dangerous) if you're in a hurry. Allow at least a half hour to drive one-way from St. Helena to Pride Mountain Vineyards, for example. All the wineries on Spring Mountain are appointment-only (thanks to a county ordinance that aims to prevent the small road from becoming too busy), but with the exception of Pride you can usually secure an appointment a day or two ahead.

Wineries by Appointment
SPRING MOUNTAIN VINEYARDS
Not far out of St. Helena is one of the oldest Spring Mountain wineries, one that is almost as famous for its Hollywood connection as for its history and wines. Established in the 1880s as the Miravalle estate, **Spring Mountain Vineyards** (2805 Spring Mountain Rd., St. Helena, 707/967-4188 or 877/769-4637, www.springmtn.com, 10am-4pm daily by appointment, tasting $25) was later used as the set for the 1980s television soap opera *Falcon Crest*. Today, Spring Mountain's vineyards stretch from the valley floor almost to the top of Spring Mountain, giving the winery a huge variety of soils and microclimates to work with. It is perhaps best known for its sauvignon blanc and cabernet sauvignon, in particular the meritage blend called Elivette, which is predominantly cabernet and gets consistently high ratings. The winery also makes a Spring Mountain syrah that has won plenty of critical praise in recent years, and, thanks to a cool spot in the mountain vineyards, it also grows and produces a few hundred cases of pinot noir, a wine not normally made this far north in the valley.

Tours ($50) of the beautiful grounds and some of the historic buildings, including its famous mansion and caves, are offered three times a day at 11am, 1pm, and 3pm by appointment. The short tours are followed by a seated tasting of four or five reserve wines. For half the price, guests can opt for the standard tasting offered every hour.

TERRA VALENTINE
One man's remarkable dedication to craftsmanship is reason alone to visit **Terra Valentine** (3787 Spring Mountain Rd., St. Helena, 707/967-8340, www.terravalentine.com, open daily by appointment, tasting $45-60). Built by the previous owner, Fred Aves, the Gothic-style drystone and concrete winery is replete with stained-glass windows (made by Aves as well),

statues, and curious features like fish-shaped doorknobs and a sculpted spiral staircase. Any home improvement aficionado will be in awe of his handiwork.

Terra Valentine still makes wine in the building and is known mainly for its cabernet sauvignon, the best of which is the flagship bottling from the Wurtele vineyard. It also makes a Russian River Valley pinot noir and a couple of limited-production wines, including a sangiovese-and-cabernet blend called Amore.

Appointment-only tours are offered twice a day (11am and 3pm); they can be on the short side depending on the time of year but are worth it to see the fabulous building and for the sit-down tasting of wines paired with cheese and chocolate.

SCHWEIGER VINEYARDS
Schweiger Vineyards (4015 Spring Mountain Rd., St. Helena, 707/963-4882 or 877/963-4882, www.schweigervineyards.com, tours and tasting by appointment 10am-4pm daily, tasting $20-30) is another of Spring Mountain's small makers of highly regarded cabernet sauvignon, and another with spectacular views from its vineyards. The vast majority of the wine is cabernet, but Schweiger also makes small amounts of merlot and chardonnay, all from the estate vineyards at about 2,000 feet in elevation, and a nice sauvignon blanc from a vineyard over the hill in the Sonoma Valley. The flagship wine is the reserve cabernet, called Dedication, which competes with the best from Spring Mountain. Another perennial favorite is the cabernet port, which is made in true nonvintage style by blending wines dating back more than a decade.

BARNETT VINEYARDS
It's a long and winding driveway leading to **Barnett Vineyards** (4070 Spring Mountain Rd., St. Helena, 707/963-7075, www.barnettvineyards.com, 10am-4pm daily by appointment, tour and tasting $40-65) from the main road, but the reward is worth the few wrong turns you might take along the way. This appointment-only boutique winery takes care to

keep guests to a minimum to ensure the wines and the tranquility of the panoramic Napa Valley view can be enjoyed in all their glory. It's one of the best views from a vineyard you'll find in this part of the world.

A visit to the winery starts at the tasting bar, tucked away in a corner of the cool dark barrel room, where most of the half-dozen wines are usually available to taste. Spring Mountain vineyards are the source of Barnett's cabernet and merlot, both of which exhibit the classic concentration and robust tannins of Spring Mountain fruit. The tangy chardonnay is sourced from southern Sonoma, and the pinot noir comes from the cool Green Valley appellation in the Russian River Valley, but it often sells out within six months of its release. Another wine that sells out fast despite its $125 price tag, probably due to the glowing reviews it gets almost every year, is the flagship Rattlesnake Hill cabernet, sourced from vines on a small knoll above the winery at 2,400 feet elevation.

If the weather is cooperating, guests can often continue tasting the wines and learn more about the winery and its vineyards on one of two small decks perched at the end of rocky paths among the terraced vineyards. You feel a little like a mountain goat traversing the terraces, and heels are not recommended. A woodburning pizza oven on the top deck might one day be pressed into action for hungry visitors, but until then the panoramic views across the Napa Valley and the almost uncanny silence are perfect accompaniments to the outstanding wines.

PRIDE MOUNTAIN VINEYARDS

When you reach the line on the road that marks the border of Napa and Sonoma Counties, you're as far up Spring Mountain as you can go and just outside the estate of **Pride Mountain Vineyards** (4026 Spring Mountain Rd., St. Helena, 707/963-4949, www.pridewines.com, 10am-3:30pm Mon. and Wed.-Sat. by appointment, tasting $10), a winery that has been receiving wine reviews almost as lofty as its location 2,000 feet up in the Mayacamas

Mountains. It is known for its powerful and intense cabernet sauvignon and merlot. Other wines that regularly score over 90 points with the critics include an aromatic cabernet franc, chardonnay, and viognier. Many Pride wines sell out quickly, particularly the limited-production reserves.

Grapes have been grown here since 1870, by some accounts, and the size of the burned-out shell of the old Summit winery building, constructed in 1890, suggests that a fair amount of wine was produced until Prohibition ended the party. The 80 acres of vineyards that Pride owns straddle the Sonoma-Napa border on these mountain ridges that afford panoramic views over the two valleys and beyond.

The views and wines are best sampled on the tour and tasting ($15) offered once a day at 10am, for which you must book well in advance even at relatively quiet times of the year. Appointment-only tastings are offered the rest of the day and cost only $10, a relative bargain considering the quality of the wines that generally cost upward of $50 a bottle and the attentive, often entertaining service. Visitors can also book picnic tables and eat at what is probably the highest picnic ground in Wine Country. With views across the vineyards to distant mountains, there's definitely a feeling of being on top of the world.

SIGHTS

Much of St. Helena's Victorian heyday is on display on Main Street (mainly between Hunt and Adams Streets), in the residential area stretching a few blocks west and just one block east on Railroad Avenue. Even the unusual street lamps on Main Street are antiques, dating from 1915.

At **1302 Main Street** (at Hunt Street), a brass inlay in the sidewalk is the only sign that the wonderfully named Wonderful Drug Store had its home for half a century in this building constructed in 1891 by local businessman Daniel Hunt (as a sign of the times, the building is now home to a clothing store and a restaurant).

North up that block is the retro-looking

Cameo Cinema (1340 Main St., 707/963-9779, www.cameocinema.com), the latest in a long line of theaters to inhabit the 1913 building with its pressed-steel ceilings and classy deco exterior, both now complemented by state-of-the-art seating, sound, and projection.

At the end of that block is the former **Odd Fellows Hall** (1350 Main St.), built in 1885 as Lodge 167 of the Independent Order of Odd Fellows, the social fraternity established in 1810 in England. The building is said to have a sealed granite memorial stone containing a time capsule of articles from the era. It was also once home to the neighboring Steves Hardware, itself founded in 1878.

Almost opposite at 1351 Main Street is what used to be the **Bank of St. Helena,** established and built in the 1880s by a group of local wine-makers, including Charles Krug. A lot of the original interior features and stone walls are still evident, though the building, until recently the 1351 Lounge, is now an olive oil store. Farther south (1305-1309 Main St.) is another 1880s building (this one made of wood) that is home to the **Hotel St. Helena** (1309 Main St., St. Helena, 707/963-4388, www.hotelsthelena.net).

Robert Louis Stevenson Silverado Museum

One of the valley's most famous literary visitors, the Scottish writer Robert Louis Stevenson, spent his honeymoon in the valley just as St. Helena's Victorian building boom was getting under way in 1880. His life and visit is celebrated in the compact **Silverado Museum** (1490 Library Ln., off Adams St., 707/963-3757, www.silveradomuseum.org, noon-4pm Tues.-Sat., free), right next to the small library a few blocks from Main Street.

There are more than 9,000 of Stevenson's personal artifacts on display, including original manuscripts of some of his many books. The most famous in these parts is *The Silverado Squatters,* published in 1883, which chronicles his Napa Valley travels and meetings with early wine industry pioneers. Stevenson is probably best known elsewhere in the world for some of his other books, including *Treasure Island* and *The Strange Case of Dr. Jekyll and Mr. Hyde.*

Also housed in the library building is the **Napa Valley Wine Library** (707/963-5244, 2pm-6pm Sun.-Mon., 10am-9pm Tues.-Thurs., 10am-6pm Fri.-Sat.). There you will find 3,500 titles and 6,000 items all related to wine in the valley and in general. It is a wonderful place to brush up on your knowledge while taking a break from tasting.

Bale Grist Mill

About three miles north of St. Helena is one of the more unusual sights in a valley dominated by the wine industry, the **Bale Grist Mill** (3369 N St. on Hwy. 29, 3 miles north of St. Helena, 707/942-4575, www.parks.ca.gov, grounds open daily, buildings 10am-5pm Sat.-Sun.). The small, rickety-looking redwood mill building with its oversized, 36-foot-high waterwheel is now part of a small State Historic Park. It was built in 1846 by Edward Bale on a tiny part of the 10,000 acres of land he was granted by the Mexican government as thanks for his role as surgeon-in-chief for the Mexican army in California (it also probably helped that he had married the niece of the army's regional commander, General Mariano Vallejo, a few years earlier).

He bartered away chunks of his land for money and services to help build both this mill and a separate sawmill not far away. It originally had a 20-foot waterwheel, but a later owner made a few power upgrades, adding the bigger wheel and iron cogs in the 1850s, a few years after Bale died. In an age of supermarkets it can be hard to see the relevance of this relic of 19th-century farming, but the mill was a major part of valley life. People came from far and wide to grind their grain, making it a major social hub long before the age of wine.

The weekend-only tours shed more light on both the man and the milling. The wheel turns sporadically these days, subject to the vagaries of its age and park budget cuts. When it is operating (usually only during the summer), there is usually some "run of the mill" flour for sale, ground between the giant millstones that literally weigh a ton. If it's not operating, the only real reason to visit (unless you're a water mill junkie) is the setting. The mill itself and a handful of picnic tables are reached from the parking lot along a quarter-mile trail that ends looping back to the main road, so traffic noise and the rather sad state of the mill building itself make for a bit of an anticlimax. Instead, turn left before reaching the mill to take the pretty mile-long hike through the madrone woods, past the remains of the valley's first church and into neighboring **Bothe-Napa Valley State Park** (3801 St. Helena Hwy. N., 707/942-4575, www.parks.ca.gov, sunrise-sunset, $8 day-use fee).

ENTERTAINMENT
◖ Culinary Institute of America
The Napa Valley takes food very seriously, so it's fitting that the West Coast outpost of the **Culinary Institute of America** (CIA, 2555 Main St., St. Helena, 707/967-2320, www.ciachef.edu, 11:30am-9pm Sun.-Thurs., 11:30am-10pm Fri.-Sat.) is housed in one of the grandest old winery buildings in California, the fortress-like former Greystone Winery just north of downtown St. Helena. Built in 1890, it later found fame as the Christian Brothers winery, but today, chefs and sommeliers are busy being trained behind the imposing stone walls.

Thankfully, you don't need the dedication they have to learn a secret or two from the Napa Valley's top chefs. Hour-long cooking demonstrations are open to the public (reservations 707/967-2320, 1:30pm weekends, $20) and include a tasting of the finished dish paired with a glass of wine, so the fee is worthwhile, especially at lunchtime. Don't expect to go more than once over a single weekend, though, because the same demonstration is given on both days.

If you're not looking for such a commitment, you can pop in at the **Bakery Café** (707/967-2320, www.ciarestaurants.com, 11am-3pm Tues.-Sat., $7) or take a seat at the highly celebrated **Wine Spectator Restaurant.** The **Spice Islands Marketplace** (707/967-2309, www.ciachef.edu, 10:30am-6pm daily) is considered

one of the best kitchen stores in the valley, supplying all those trainee chefs and sommeliers (and you) with the best culinary equipment, spices, and other essentials from around the world. You can even test your palate. Just sidle up to the **Flavor Bar** ($10-15) and enjoy one of the scheduled chocolate, cheese, and olive oil tastings.

Or you can just explore the historic building and grounds on your own. A small exhibit just beyond the huge, carved redwood entrance doors illustrates the history of the Greystone Winery with some of the original Christian Brothers barrels, casks, and brandy-making stills. Most intriguing of all is a display of more than a thousand corkscrews, some of them hundreds of years old and miniature marvels of engineering, all collected by Brother Timothy, a wine chemist and renowned winemaker at Christian Brothers 1935-1989. The organic herb and vegetable garden is also worth a visit.

Nightlife
It might seem like this part of the valley goes to sleep after the restaurants have closed down for the evening, and sadly that's more or less true. But if you're looking for a little late-night fun, join the locals at the casual hangout **Ana's Cantina** (1205 Main St., 707/963-4921, 10am-2am daily). It's a Mexican restaurant by day and a bar by night, when beer and margaritas are the drinks of choice, and pool, karaoke, and live weekend music provide the entertainment, usually until 1am. Although the bartenders know how to mix some good cocktails, this falls just shy of being a dive bar, so don't expect to see much, if any, of the usual "Wine Country" ambience. A bit more polished, **La Condesa** (1320 Main St., 707/967-8111, www.lacondesa.com, 11:30am-10pm daily) has recently gotten into the party scene. The restaurant features live music in its festive interior on the occasional weekend nights. The 200-plus mescals and tequilas behind the bar help to lubricate the fun.

For those interested in more of a Wine Country block party, plan on visiting St. Helena the first Friday of the month

May-October, where, 5:30pm-8:30pm, the local wineries offer free tastes, restaurants pass out gourmet hors d'oeuvres, shops stay open late, and live music keeps things jumping.

SHOPPING

It's hardly surprising in a valley that was built on the guilty pleasures of consumption that shopping is a close third to eating and drinking for many visitors. The short stretch of Main Street in downtown St. Helena is quick and easy to explore, with an eclectic mix of shops that draw crowds and help create some horrendous traffic jams as visitors look for parking.

Countless gift shops sell everything from soap to wine trinkets, but gifts with a global edge can be found at **Baksheesh Fair Trade** (1327 Main St., St. Helena, 707/968-9182, http://baksheeshfairtrade.com, 10am-6pm daily). Scarves and necklaces of all styles and colors fill the walls, while tall shelves showcase quirky goods, such as coasters, handbags, and even Christmas ornaments. All are made out of recycled and reclaimed materials by artisans from far-flung places like India, Peru, and Kenya, many of whose bio you can read about in the store or on the store's website. If you are looking for a feel-good purchase, this is the place to go.

Whether you have a green thumb or not, swing by **Acres Home and Garden** (1219 Main St., St. Helena, 707/967-1142, http://acreshomeandgarden.com, 10am-5pm daily). Not only will you find the most beautiful trowel and gardening gloves you've ever seen, but this slender shop also has a beautiful selection of delicate silver and gold jewelry, sumptuous soaps and candles, the quirkiest handcrafted gifts, and the most perfect array of cut flowers filling the back of the store.

While St. Helena is dominated by small boutiques that tend to cater to tourists, high-end contemporary art and design is gradually supplanting the more traditional Wine Country paraphernalia. Two of the best examples sit side by side in the historic Independent Order of Odd Fellows building on Main Street. The **Martin Showroom** (1350 Main St., St. Helena,

the Martin Showroom

© ELIZABETH LINHART VENEMAN

707/967-8787, www.martinshowroom.com, 10am-6pm Tues.-Sat.) is a showcase for designer Erin Martin, who fashions contemporary pieces with a rustic or industrial chic from natural and reclaimed materials. While you may not take home a $15,000 table or bronze statue as a souvenir of the Wine Country, there is nonetheless plenty of inspiration on offer from the works of Erin and a handful of other artists and designers represented here, along with plenty of more-affordable, whimsical items for sale, from jewelry to housewares.

Right next door is the St. Helena outpost of the **I Wolk Gallery** (1354 Main St., St. Helena, 707/963-8800, www.iwolkgallery.com, 10am-5:30pm daily), which is represented at four locations in the Napa Valley, including Maisonary in Yountville and at the Auberge du Soleil resort. Unlike the Martin showroom, this is a more traditional gallery with rotating exhibitions of contemporary works from Bay Area artists and sculptors.

Foodies might drool on entering the only West Coast outpost of New York's super-deli

Dean & Deluca (607 St. Helena Hwy. S., St. Helena, 707/967-9980, www.deandeluca.com, 7am-7pm Sun.-Thurs., 7am-8pm Fri.-Sat.), just south of downtown St. Helena. This being the Wine Country, of course, it stocks some 1,400 wines plus countless local cheeses, meats, and produce, all alongside the already unmatched selection of gourmet foods from around the world.

Chocoholics might get a sugar rush just by looking at the neat rows of dozens of hand-made bonbons at **Woodhouse Chocolate** (1367 Main St., St. Helena, 707/963-8413 or 800/966-3468, www.woodhousechocolate. com, 10:30am-5:30pm daily). It's a good old-fashioned chocolatier with interior decorations as sumptuous as the confectioneries made by Tracy Wood Anderson, a former pastry chef. Indulging is not as expensive as you'd think, particularly in this valley of pricey wine tasting. For less than a flight of wines at a local winery, you can walk out of here with a small box of chocolate bliss.

The best olive oil in town is undoubtedly at the **Napa Valley Olive Oil Manufacturing Company** (835 Charter Oak Ave., St. Helena, 707/963-4173, 9am-5:30pm daily), though it no longer presses its oils here. Despite being in the heart of the valley's food scene, it retains a decidedly small-time family feeling, selling its organic oils and thoroughly Italian deli items out of a small, colorful and chaotic barnlike store.

RECREATION

The Napa Valley might seem to be covered with vineyards, but around its fringes there are still hundreds of acres as yet untouched by the mighty vine, some only minutes away from the Wine Country hordes.

◖ Bothe-Napa Valley State Park

Just a few miles north of St. Helena and right off the main highway, **Bothe-Napa Valley State Park** (3801 St. Helena Hwy. N., 707/942-4575, www.parks.ca.gov, sunrise-sunset, $8 day-use fee) is the most accessible place up-valley to escape anything

wine related and also the inside of the car. Proximity to the wineries and shops of St. Helena makes the park a popular picnic spot, but most people packing a lunch don't venture far beyond the shady picnic area just beyond the parking lot near the Pioneer Cemetery (and the road). They miss the best reason to come here, which is to experience the relative wilderness that's so close to the beaten path and home to some of the most easterly stands of coastal redwood trees.

Most of the best hiking trails start from the **Redwood Trail,** which runs from the main parking lot through the cool redwood forest along Ritchey Creek for just over a mile before meeting the **Ritchey Canyon Trail.** That trail more or less follows the creek for about another mile to the site of an old homestead, an ideal destination for adventurous picnickers.

More strenuous hikes start from the Redwood Trail and climb steeply into the heat to some rewarding lookout points. The closest is Coyote Peak, accessed via the **Coyote Peak Trail** and just under a mile from the creek. From the lookout spur, the trail continues to the **South Fork Trail.** Turn right here to head back down to the creek for a loop of about four miles, or go left to climb again to another lookout. These trails are not for the faint-hearted, especially in the summer when it can get very hot, so don't underestimate the dehydrating power of too many glasses of wine.

Mountain bikers (or anyone on a Wine Country bike tour tired of dodging weaving rental cars) also have a few miles of trails to explore here, but only those that start north of the creek near the campground.

Golf

There are a couple of nine-hole golf courses up-valley, but serious golfers should head south to the Napa area, where all the valley's 18-hole courses are. The **Meadowood Country Club & Resort** (900 Meadowood Ln., off Silverado Trail, St. Helena, 707/963-3646, www.meadowood.com) has a nine-hole par-62 course open only to guests or guests of guests of this exclusive 250-acre hideaway.

ACCOMMODATIONS

St. Helena has a far wider range of accommodations than Calistoga, but at far higher prices, justified perhaps by the convenient location in the middle of the valley, the pretty Main Street, the thriving restaurant scene, or maybe simply because, in world-famous St. Helena, they can get away with it.

Prices are all relative, of course. The cheapest accommodations in this area might be pricier than the low end in either Napa or Calistoga, but don't expect that extra money to buy more luxury. The low end of this scale is the same as the low end on any other scale, where rooms will generally be clean and comfortable but not as luxurious as their price might suggest. At the other end of the scale are some truly luxurious rooms but at prices that might make you choke on a glass of cabernet, especially on summer weekends.

Under $150

The 1940s-era **El Bonita Motel** (195 Main St., St. Helena, 707/963-3216 or 800/541-3284, www.elbonita.com, $150), with its retro neon sign, is not the most glamorous place to stay in St. Helena but is one of the cheaper options and still pretty fancy for a motel. The Poolside rooms, laid out around a small pool and hot tub, are definitely the cheapest and suffer from less privacy and more road noise than the Homestead and Garden rooms, which are set farther back on the property and are quieter but less of a bargain, though many have kitchenettes to make up for it. All contain modern but fairly sparse furnishings and include air-conditioning, refrigerators, and microwave ovens.

$150-250

The **Hotel St. Helena** (1309 Main St., St. Helena, 707/963-4388, www.hotelsthelena. net) is about as central as can be, down a little alley off Main Street right in the middle of town. The old Victorian building is full of original features and stuffed with knickknacks, including a lot of dolls. The 18 guest rooms get some of the same treatment (minus the dolls), with brass beds, a smattering of antiques,

plush carpeting and fabrics, but limited modern touches—air-conditioning is included, but you'll have to ask for a TV. You might also have to tolerate some less charming Victorian traits such as temperamental plumbing and poor sound insulation. The four smallest and cheapest rooms share a bathroom and run $105 midweek, $195 weekends. The best deals are the North Wing rooms, which are still on the small side but have private bathrooms and start at $145 midweek, $235 weekends. The larger Windsor rooms start at $165 midweek, $275 weekends, and the single suite starts at $250 midweek, $375 weekends.

Right next to El Bonita Motel is the **Vineyard Country Inn** (201 Main St., St. Helena, 707/963-1000, www.vineyardcountryinn.com, $250), a combination of hotel and motel with 21 spacious suites that all cost the same, ranging from a relative bargain of $185 in winter months to less of a bargain at $325 during peak summer and fall seasons. All are in a main two-story building or several cottages around the pool and pleasant brick patios—just be sure to ask for a room away from the main road, which is noisy enough to render the balconies of some suites next to useless. All suites have either two queens or one king bed, vaulted or beamed ceilings, fireplaces, refrigerators, and comfortable but unexceptional country-style furniture.

One of the more reasonably priced B&Bs in the area is **Ink House** (1575 S. St. Helena Hwy., St. Helena, 707/963-3890, www.inkhouseinn.com, $200), an 1884 Victorian just south of town with an unusual observatory room perched on top of the roof, where guests can sip wine and watch the world (and the wine train) go by. The common areas are chock-full of unusual antiques, from the grand piano and pipe organ to the stained glass in the observatory. The six bedrooms continue the theme and have been lovingly decorated with a mix of antiques, and most have a view of either hills or vineyards. Rates include a full gourmet breakfast, an afternoon wine social, complimentary nightcaps, and loaner bicycles. The inn also offers a lounge area where guests may play pool or throw darts, and outside, play a round of croquet or horseshoes. To get you out the door, Winery VIP tasting passes are complimentary at the front desk.

For some true peace and quiet, skip the valley floor and head for the hills. Northeast of St. Helena near the small community of Deer Park is secluded **Spanish Villa Inn** (474 Glass Mountain Rd., St. Helena, 707/963-7483, www.napavalleyspanishvilla.com, $225), a small Mediterranean-style B&B set in several acres of beautifully tended grounds with bocce and croquet courts as well as roses galore. There are six rooms and two suites. All have private bathrooms and unusual touches like hand-painted sinks, plantation-style shutters, and carved headboards but, alas, an overabundance of floral prints. Downstairs rooms open onto a patio overlooking the garden, while one of the upstairs suites has its own balcony. None accommodate pets or children.

Over $250

On the southern edge of St. Helena, hidden from the road behind a thicket of trees, is the mock-Tudor mansion of the **Harvest Inn** (1 Main St., St. Helena, 707/963-9463 or 800/950-8466, www.harvestinn.com, $450), set in eight acres of lush gardens shaded by mature trees. The place is crammed with stylish antiques, fancy brickwork, and other often-surreal English country features. There's nothing surreal about the luxury of the 74 rooms and suites, however: All have CD players and VCRs, featherbeds, and minibars; some have their own private terrace or views of neighboring vineyards. If that isn't enough, the grounds include two outside heated swimming pools, a wine bar, spa, and fitness center.

Its location surrounded by vineyards a few miles north of St. Helena makes the **Wine Country Inn** (1152 Lodi Ln., St. Helena, 707/963-7077 or 888/465-4608, www.winecountryinn.com, $350) a slightly cheaper alternative to some of the other luxury resorts out in the wilds. This family-run establishment offers an unusual down-home atmosphere, good amenities, and a decent breakfast. Rooms are

decorated with a mix of modern and rustic; CD players and handmade quilts enhance the sometimes simple furniture. You'll either love the combination or wonder why you're paying so much, but splurge on a room with a view, and there'll be no questioning it. There are a variety of rooms (and prices) to choose from. The smallest rooms start at $240, but rooms with views or a private patio tick up the cost. Small suites with added features like balconies with a view, whirlpool tubs, and double-headed showers are also available, as are five luxury cottages with 800 square feet of lounging space.

The luxurious **Meadowood Napa Valley** (900 Meadowood Ln., off Silverado Trail, St. Helena, 707/531-4788 or 877/963-3646, www.meadowood.com, $550) resort is facing increasing competition in this astronomical price bracket, but it's still worth considering if you're planning to splurge, not least because of its spectacular setting on 250 lush acres in the hills above the Silverado Trail. The rooms are in 20 country-style lodges spread around the grounds and range from simple two-room studios up to spacious suites. All have fireplaces, beamed ceilings, private decks or terraces, and every conceivable luxury trapping. For those who actually venture out of the rooms, there are plenty of distractions, including miles of hiking trails, two swimming pools surrounded by vast expanses of lawn, tennis courts, a nine-hole golf course, and croquet. And to make sure visitors never have to venture down into the valley, there's a small spa, wine-tasting events, and two highly regarded restaurants on-site.

Camping

The Napa Valley might be touted by every marketing brochure as a bank-breaking hedonistic playground, but it actually has a couple of remarkably good campgrounds where two people can stay for less than it would cost them to taste wine at most of the nearby wineries. So forget about matching a Napa cabernet with an entrées at the latest Michelin-starred restaurant—instead see how it goes with s'mores around a campfire under a warm summer night sky.

You can light your fire and unpack the

marshmallows just a few miles north of St. Helena in the leafy **Bothe-Napa Valley State Park** (3801 St. Helena Hwy. N., 707/942-4575, www.parks.ca.gov). There are 50 sites, 42 of which can accommodate RVs up to 31 feet long (though there are no hookups). The other eight sites are tent-only, and all cost $35 per night. Sites can be reserved April-October through Reserve America (www.reserveamerica.com or 800/444-7275). Most sites offer some shade beneath oak and madrone trees, and there's a swimming pool, which may or may not be open on the weekends, in which to cool off, as well as flush toilets, hot showers, and that all-important fire ring at every site. The park itself stretches up into the hills and offers miles of hiking trails through the redwoods along the creek or up into the sun for some great views.

FOOD

There's an ongoing tug-of-war between up-valley and down-valley restaurants for the limited tourist food dollars, and the balance seems to shift almost every time one restaurant closes and a new one opens—both common occurrences in the Napa Valley. St. Helena's ever-changing restaurant scene with its big-name chefs continues to do battle with towns down south, competing with Yountville for the title of Napa Valley's culinary epicenter.

California Cuisine

Typically, one of the first things that happen when you sit down at a restaurant is a server hands you a menu; at **The Restaurant at Meadowood** (900 Meadowood Ln., 707/967-1205, www.therestaurantatmeadowood.com, 5:30pm-10pm Mon.-Sat., $225) it comes at the end of the meal, with your name on it. Garnering three Michelin stars (the only other in Northern California is The French Laundry) two years in a row, Meadowood is the talk of the St. Helena dining scene. For $225 (wine pairing is extra), diners are treated to a nine-course tasting menu carefully crafted by chef Christopher Kostow, whose approach to food is a combination of farm-to-table ethos executed with French precision. Diners will be surprised by sumptuous bites of duck with persimmon and maple, fermented pear puree and seared sturgeon, Asian pear soda served with warm frankincense sabayon, and the list goes on and on. Despite the haute cuisine, the restaurant works hard to maintain a reasonably relaxed atmosphere (clean dark denim pants are okay!), and the deep black leather chairs and more than adequate spacing between the tables make the space itself exceedingly comfortable. What you may not be as comfortable about is how far in advance you need to make a reservation (three months) or the many questions you're asked once you do (your name, the names of all your guests, and any dietary restrictions or preferences). The cancellation policy may make you downright queasy: 48 hours' notice or your credit card will be charged $225 per person.

Another Michelin-starred favorite is **Terra** (1345 Railroad Ave., St. Helena, 707/963-8931, www.terrasrestaurant.com, 6pm-9:30pm Wed.-Mon., entrées $20-36), located in the historic stone Hatchery Building. A romantic restaurant, it competes with the best restaurants in the valley (with its food and spin-off cookbook) thanks to chef Hiro Sone, who won the prestigious James Beard Foundation award for Best Chef in California. The menu is French and Californian with Asian flourishes, and might include such eclectic creations as sake-marinated Alaskan black cod with shrimp dumplings. Diners create their own prix fix by selecting four ($70), five ($85) or six ($97) courses from the 17 savory dishes on the menu. For something more casual but with the same fusion flare, step to the right at the entrance and dine at **Bar Terra.** With a full liquor license and an à la carte menu ($13-22), you can nibble on any one of Terra's signature dishes for considerably less.

Practically next door on Railroad Avenue is **C Cindy's Backstreet Kitchen** (1327 Railroad Ave., St. Helena, 707/963-1200, www.cindysbackstreetkitchen.com, 11:30am-9pm Sun.-Thurs., 11:30am-9:30 Fri.-Sat., $20). The Cindy is Cindy Pawlcyn, who is largely credited with bringing casual yet sophisticated dining to the Napa Valley when she opened Younville's Mustards Grill in 1983. Done with her usual panache, her "backstreet" kitchen feels just that: a charming hole-in-the-wall with a side entrance that makes it feel like you're walking into someone's house. The menu goes for the same homey charm, with large plates including meatloaf, wood-oven duck, and *steak frites*. The small plates and sandwiches for lunch can be ordered to go. Be aware, however, that the quiet patio is a hive of activity at lunchtime and can require a wait. If the line is too long, Pawlcyn's latest venture, **Cindy Pawlcyn's Wood Grill and Wine Bar** (641 Main St., St. Helena, 707/963-0700, http://cindypawlcynsgrill.com, 11:30am-9:30pm Sun. and Wed.-Thurs., 11:30am-10pm Fri.-Sat., $22) is a revamp of her recently closed Go Fish and cooks Wine Country comfort food that is inventive and solid. One perk is the Vintner Splash (6pm-8:30pm every Sat.), in which one winemaker is invited to pour a complimentary "splash" of their wine to diners.

Almost opposite Cindy Pawlcyn's Wood Grill and Wine Bar is **Farmstead** (738 Main St., St. Helena, 707/963-9181, 11:30am-9:30pm Mon.-Thurs., 11:30am-10pm Fri.-Sat., 11am-9:30pm Sun., $22), which takes the idea of farm-fresh to a new level. It is run by the Long Meadow Ranch (707/963-4555, www.longmeadowranch.com), a winery and farm based in the hills above Rutherford that supplies many of the ingredients, including vegetables, herbs, olive oil, eggs, and grass-fed beef (a specialty). The rustic restaurant is housed in the barn of the former Whiting Nursery, where salvaged farm equipment and even old tree stumps have found new life as fixtures, fittings, and furnishings. Even the booths are covered in leather sourced from the ranch's cattle. Complementing the atmosphere, the food hits just the right balance of sophistication and familiarity. If none of the well-priced wines in the varied California-heavy wine list appeals, the restaurant imposes only a $2 charitable donation to open a bottle of your own. To escape the echo-chamber noise in the barn, ask for one of the coveted tables on the outdoor patio surrounded by fruit trees.

Another solid choice, and one where you might be able to bypass the reservation line, is **Market** (1347 Main St., St. Helena, 707/963-3799, www.marketsthelena.com, 11:30am-9pm Mon.-Thurs., 11:30am-10pm Fri.-Sat., 10am-9pm Sun., dinner entrées $12-24). The American bistro-style food is sophisticated yet familiar, with dishes like pan-roasted crispy chicken sharing the menu with mac and cheese made, of course, with the best artisanal cheeses. The stone walls, Victorian bar, and elegant tables might suggest an astronomical bill at the end of your meal, but instead the prices and atmosphere are very down-to-earth, and jaded locals have grown to love the place. The wine list manages to keep a lid on prices, with none of the wide selection more than $14 above retail, beating even the corkage fee of most local restaurants. The lunch menu is even more of a bargain, with most of the gourmet sandwiches and salads under $16. All are also available to go, providing an instant gourmet picnic.

Goose and Gander (1245 Spring St., 707/967-8779, www.goosegander.com, noon-midnight daily, $22) channels the cocktail driven, meaty farm-fresh cuisine, faux turn-of-the-20th-century aesthetic that has colored the San Francisco dining scene over the last couple of years. Here, at the location of the once popular Martini House, the low-lit interior is warmed with dark wood, back-tufted leather booths, and a deep bar that showcases a stable of high-caliber, hard-to-find spirits that are made into cocktails self-labeled as "retro-fresh." If you're detouring from wine, this is the place to order a Manhattan. Thankfully, the menu is tailored around a highball. Plates of cheese, charcuterie, or dishes of roasted bone marrow, pork sugo, and cioppino keep tipsy stomachs full.

Italian

Tra Vigne (1050 Charter Oak Ave., St. Helena, 707/963-4444, www.travignerestaurant.com, 11:30am-9pm Mon.-Sat., 11am-9pm Sun., $18-30) is a rarity in the valley—a restaurant that has been around since the early 1990s without ever really changing its formula (it has changed chefs a few times, however). This is a thoroughly Italian place with a classic Italian American menu, lots of cool stone and terracotta tile, and a wonderful enclosed leafy patio straight out of Tuscany. The wine list reflects the California-inspired Italian menu, with a good selection of local and Italian wines to go with the exquisite pizzas, pastas, and dinner entrées prepared with the usual high-quality local ingredients.

If getting a reservation at Tra Vigne is a problem, you can still experience its winning formula at **Pizzeria Tra Vigne** (1016 Main St., St. Helena, 707/967-9999, www.travignerestaurant.com, 11:30am-9pm Sun.-Thurs., 11:30am-9:30pm Fri.-Sat., $9-18), where the huge wood-fired oven sits center stage. From it come the famous thin-crust Italian pizzas that lure locals on many weekend nights. You can also get hearty plates of pasta or heavy Italian salads, and servers are happy to deliver pitchers of any number of beers they have on tap. There are also a number of beers by the bottle, in addition to a healthy selection of wine. If you're traveling with kids, Pizzeria Tra Vigne is a great place to stop and relax over a meal. They even have a pool table.

St. Helenians may be spoiled with noteworthy restaurants, but when you ask the locals, "Where do you go?," they will invariably say, **Cook St. Helena** (1310 Main St., St. Helena, 707/963-7088, www.cooksthelena.com, 11:30am-10pm Mon.-Sat., 5pm-10pm Sun., $25). This slender restaurant, painted in steel blue and accented with dark wood and white linen, serves classic rustic Italian-style food. You'll find linguine with clams, pappardelle with pork, braised lamb, and seared flat iron steak; a healthy Napa-centric wine list; and a full bar with fresh and inventive cocktails. While this is not one of the big Napa Valley tourist draws, reservations are recommended.

Mexican

Want a flavorful, south-of-the-border lunch to go with an afternoon of window shopping on Main Street? The fun, brightly painted **La Condesa** (1320 Main St., St. Helena, 707/967-8111, www.lacondesa.com, 11:30am-10pm daily, $14) is the place to go. Like any other place worth its salt in the valley, La Condesa contracts with a local farm to supply its fresh, Mexican-inspired menu created and executed by Chris Mortenson, a veteran of Mexican cuisine for over 20 years. On his menu you'll find tacos made with soft house-made tortillas, refined small plates such as raw yellowtail with pickled cucumber on a crispy tostadita, or specialties rarely found outside of Mexico—like Huitlacoche Huarache, a mushroom and corn dish. You can wash down your spicy lunch with wine or beer, or if you're feeling more adventurous, you can opt for a flight of La Condesa's 200 tequilas or mezcals. Even if you're not quite up for it, hang onto the drink menu; the tasting notes are a fun read.

Cafés and Bakeries

The **Model Bakery** (1357 Main St., St. Helena, 707/963-8192, www.themodelbakery.com, 6:30am-5:30pm Mon.-Fri., 7am-5:30pm Sat., 7am-5pm Sun., lunch items $4-10) is known for baking some of the best bread in the valley and is the latest incarnation of a bakery that has existed here since the 1920s. It's a great place for quick and easy lunches, including gourmet sandwiches, salads, and pizza cooked in the same brick ovens as the bread. Most can be ordered to go, but you might also be lucky enough to snag one of the few tables dotted around the black-and-white-tiled floor like strategically placed chess pieces.

If quick refreshment is all you need to keep going, the **Napa Valley Coffee Roasting Company** (1400 Oak Ave., St. Helena, 707/963-4491, www.napavalleycoffee.com, 7am-8pm Mon.-Fri., 7:30am-8pm Sat.-Sun.) offers some peace and quiet on its patio a block from Main Street.

Casual Dining

For the best breakfasts and no-nonsense lunches in St. Helena, head to **Gillwoods Café** (1313 Main St., St. Helena, 707/963-1788,

La Condesa

7am-3pm daily, most dishes $10). It's a friendly, no-frills diner popular with locals and perfect for some good old-fashioned hearty food to prepare you for a day of exploring or to help you recover from yesterday's overconsumption of wine.

Although St. Helena's food scene is constantly changing, there is one place that the term "institution" could apply to, and that's the half-century-old **Gott's Roadside** (933 Main St., St. Helena, 707/963-3486, www.gottsroadside.com, 10:30am-9pm daily in winter, 10:30am-10pm daily in summer, $10), formerly Taylor's Automatic Refresher. This unmistakable old diner just south of downtown is home of the ahi burger and other diner delights, many given a Wine Country gourmet twist but also with prices that have been given a Wine Country lift. A big grassy picnic area with plenty of tables gives a little respite from the traffic, or perch on a stool at the counter. It's a unique experience, but after dropping $30 or more for lunch for two people in the summer, and waiting in a long line for

the restrooms, you might wish you'd gone to a more traditional restaurant with more traditional air-conditioning and facilities. More civilized outposts of Gott's have opened in Napa and San Francisco, but this is the original and still the best if you want some old-school kid-friendly outdoor fun.

Picnic Supplies

The ease of finding picnic food in this part of the valley is matched only by the ease of finding a place to eat it, whether at the countless wineries with big and small patches of grass or among the redwoods in the Bothe-Napa Valley State Park.

Several of St. Helena's restaurants offer almost all their lunch menu items to go, including **Cindy's Backstreet Kitchen, Market, Farmstead,** and the **Model Bakery.** But even they cannot compete with the gourmet paradise of **Dean & Deluca** (607 St. Helena Hwy. S., St. Helena, 707/967-9980, www.deandeluca.com, 7am-7pm Sun.-Thurs., 7am-8pm Fri.-Sat.). Just don't lose track of time while browsing the food you never knew existed. A cheaper and altogether quirkier place to buy sandwiches is the old-fashioned deli counter at **Giugni's Grocery & Deli** (1227 Main St., St. Helena, 707/963-3421, 9am-4:30pm daily), an old St. Helena institution that's chock-full of fascinating family memorabilia. Be sure to ask for some Giugni juice, a trademark marinade that's delicious. Those planning to build their own sandwich can also battle through the crowds to the well-stocked deli at the **V. Sattui Winery** (1111 White Ln., St. Helena, 707/963-7774, www.vsattui.com, 9am-5pm daily).

And don't shun the ugly strip-mall home of **Sunshine Foods** (1115 Main St., St. Helena, 707/963-7070, 7:30am-8:30pm daily), next to the Wells Fargo bank at the southern end of the downtown zone. It's a quality grocery store with a remarkably broad range of deli sandwiches and salads, wines, and even freshly made sushi.

Farmers Market
The place to buy local produce direct from the farmers is the **St. Helena Farmers Market** (7:30am-noon Fri. May-Oct.), held at Crane Park west of Main Street; access is via Sulphur Springs Road or Mills Lane.

INFORMATION AND SERVICES
The **St. Helena Welcome Center** (657 Main St., 707/963-4456, www.sthelena.com, 9am-5pm Mon.-Fri., 10am-5pm Sat.-Sun.) has maps, information, and discounted wine-tasting vouchers. Thankfully, there is parking in the back; turn on Vidovich Lane just north of the visitors center.

If you're in town for a few days, the local **St. Helena Star** (http://napavalleyregister.com/star) is worth picking up at any local café, as much for the latest Wine Country gossip as for information about local events and some entertaining wine-related columns.

For any health concerns, the **St. Helena Hospital** (10 Woodland Rd., 707/963-6425, http://sthelenanowaiter.org) has a 24-hour emergency room that provides quick and reliable service.

To mail a letter, the **post office** (1461 Main St.) is located at between Pine and Adams Streets. If you need to withdraw some cash, there is a **Wells Fargo** (1107 Main St.) and a **Bank of America** (1001 Adams St.).

GETTING THERE AND AROUND
The next town north on Highway 29 after Rutherford, St. Helena is in the center of the valley and only eight miles south of Calistoga. To jump over to the Silverado Trail, take Zinfandel Lane or Pope Street east.

If you want to avoid the constant headache of parking and driving in traffic around town, consider hopping aboard **The St. Helena VINE Shuttle** (707/963-3007, http://nctpa.net, 7:45am-5pm Mon.-Fri., $0.50-1). The only problem is that it doesn't run on the weekends when traffic is really rotten.

Like elsewhere in the valley, the St. Helena area is great to explore by bike. Right downtown is the **St. Helena Cyclery** (1156 Main St., 707/963-7736, www.sthelenacyclery.com, 9:30am-5:30pm Tues.-Sat., 10am-5pm Sun.), which rents basic hybrid bikes for $15 per hour or $39 per day and more advanced road bikes from $70 per day but only takes reservations for groups of 10 or more. Check the website for coupons and other specials. You can also rent bikes at **Velo Vino** (709 Main St., St. Helena, 707/968-0625, www.cliffamilywinery.com, 10am-6pm daily), which has a partnership with Calistoga Bike Shop. Road bikes are available for $100 per day, while cruisers can be rented for a half ($45) or full ($60) day. While you are arranging your tour, the folks at the tasting counter will help you plan your route, pour you an espresso, and sell you any Clif family snacks for the road.

Calistoga

No other town in the Napa Valley retains a sense of its pioneer Victorian roots more than Calistoga, with the remaining stretch of its old boardwalk and Victorian storefronts framed by views in all directions of mountains and forests. Replace the cars and paving with horses and mud, and things would probably look much like they did a hundred years ago when the spa town was at its peak, drawing visitors from far and wide to its natural hot springs and mud baths.

The town was built on mud, literally and figuratively. San Francisco businessman Sam Brannan bought up thousands of acres of land here in the 1850s, drawn by the development potential of the hot springs. He opened a very profitable general store in the late 1850s (now a historic landmark at 203 Wapoo Ave.), followed by his lavish Hot Springs Resort in 1868. He was also instrumental in bringing the railroad this far up the valley to transport visitors to his new resort, making the town a destination for the masses and a gateway to Sonoma and Lake Counties to the north.

What Brannan is perhaps best known for, however, is an alcohol-induced slip of the tongue. Legend has it that in a speech promoting his resort he planned to say that it would become known as the "Saratoga of California," referring to the famous New York spa town, but his words instead came out as the "Calistoga of Sarafornia."

Perhaps more than any other valley town, all this history does not seem that far away, but Calistoga is not preserved in amber. The funky town is the most affordable place to live in the valley, and its population (and its relatively large Latino population) reflects that. While wine is certainly the main economic engine, here Calistogans are not easily wooed by the promise of big resorts such as farther down-valley. While most agree that the Solage resort has been a boon, two more big resorts (one on Diamond Mountain) are in the planning phase

and are being met with considerable resistance by Calistoga stalwarts, creating friction between members of the community.

The Wines

Many visitors never really explore the wineries this far north in the valley, and they are missing out. Not only are the crowds thinner (and the food cheaper), but this area also was a historic hub of winemaking in the valley. There's still plenty of winemaking action at both small boutique wineries and grand architectural palaces. The area's latest claim to fame is the impressive Tuscan castle built by valley son Dario Sattui just south of Calistoga.

Although the Calistoga area was one of the first places that grapes were grown in the Napa Valley, it has been one of the last to be granted its own sub-appellation status. Chateau Montelena led the charge to get the **Calistoga** AVA officially designated, and the process took far longer than anticipated, but finally, in December 2009, after six years, the "Battle of Calistoga" was won, and the area became the 15th AVA in the Napa Valley. One reason it took so long is that a nearby winery called Calistoga Cellars had not been using grapes from the region in its wine, so would be unable to continue using the word "Calistoga" on its labels. It tried and failed to get an exception to the labeling rule, and must now either change its name or start buying local grapes.

On the western slopes, home of the historic Schramsberg winery and the pseudo-historic Castello di Amorosa, is the **Diamond Mountain** AVA. It was designated in 2001 as the first sub-appellation in the northern part of the Napa Valley. Winemakers there are already making a name for Diamond Mountain wines as they learn to tame and soften the powerful tannins of the mountain grapes to create increasingly impressive and intense wines with trademark hints of dark chocolate.

Not many white-wine grapes are grown on

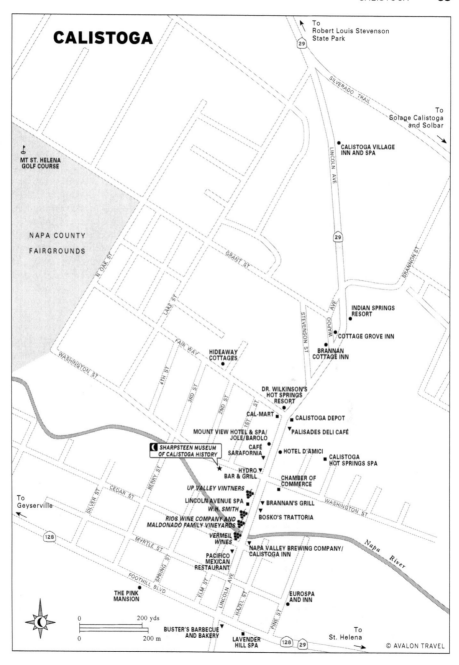

CALISTOGA

To
Robert Louis Stevenson
State Park
(29)

SILVERADO TRAIL

To
Solage Calistoga
and Solbar

MT ST. HELENA
GOLF COURSE

NAPA COUNTY
FAIRGROUNDS

CALISTOGA VILLAGE
INN AND SPA

LINCOLN AVE

(29)

N OAK ST

GRANT ST

LAKE ST

STEVENSON ST

WAPOO AVE

BRANNON ST

INDIAN SPRINGS
RESORT

COTTAGE GROVE INN

FAIR WAY

4TH ST

3RD ST

2ND ST

HIDEAWAY
COTTAGES

BRANNAN
COTTAGE INN

WASHINGTON ST

DR. WILKINSON'S
HOT SPRINGS
RESORT

CAL-MART

1ST ST

CALISTOGA DEPOT

PALISADES DELI CAFÉ

MOUNT VIEW HOTEL & SPA/
JOLE/BAROLO

CAFÉ
SARAFORNIA

HOTEL D'AMICI

CALISTOGA
HOT SPRINGS SPA

BERRY ST

SHARPSTEEN MUSEUM
OF CALISTOGA HISTORY

HYDRO
BAR & GRILL

CHAMBER OF
COMMERCE

To
Geyserville

CEDAR ST

SILVER ST

UP VALLEY VINTNERS

LINCOLN AVENUE SPA

W.H. SMITH

BRANNAN'S GRILL

WASHINGTON ST

(128)

RIOS WINE COMPANY AND
MALDONADO FAMILY VINEYARDS

BOSKO'S TRATTORIA

MYRTLE ST

SPRING ST

VERMEIL
WINES

Napa   River

PACIFICO
MEXICAN
RESTAURANT

NAPA VALLEY BREWING COMPANY/
CALISTOGA INN

FOOTHILL BLVD

ELM ST

LINCOLN AVE

HAZEL ST

THE PINK
MANSION

EUROSPA
AND INN

PINE ST

0   200 yds

0   200 m

BUSTER'S BARBECUE
AND BAKERY

LAVENDER
HILL SPA

To
St. Helena

(128)(29)

© AVALON TRAVEL

Diamond Mountain, but on the valley floor, in the Calistoga AVA, whites are common and as impressive as anywhere else in the valley, while the reds have an intensity and power indicative of the warm climate this far up-valley. Indeed, Calistoga temperatures in the summer are often a good 20 degrees warmer than down in Carneros, and nights are not nearly as cold, creating ripening conditions closer to those in Sonoma's Alexander Valley than in some parts of the Napa Valley.

CALISTOGA AREA WINERIES

FRANK FAMILY VINEYARDS

The imposing sandstone building of the historic Larkmead Winery (1091 Larkmead Ln., Calistoga, 707/942-0859 or 800/574-9463, www.frankfamilyvineyards.com, 10am-5pm daily, tasting $20-30), a few miles south of Calistoga, has had a more colorful history than most, finding fame for still and sparkling wines as well as surviving many identities and a big fire in 2000 that destroyed an estimated 85,000 cases. The winery was founded in 1884, but eventually divided in 1948; the majority of the vineyards became the Larkmead Vineyards (across the street). The winery itself became **Frank Family Vineyards** when the property was bought by Hollywood executive Rich Frank in 1992. In its current incarnation it is perhaps as well known for an unpretentious and slightly quirky tasting experience as for its wines.

The winery makes about 15,000 cases of still and sparkling wines. The increasing emphasis is on still wines, particularly cabernet sauvignon from Rutherford-area vineyards and pinot noir from Carneros. Sparkling wine remains an important part of the portfolio, however, and a dry blanc de blancs is offered as the first part of the tasting in the tasting room in the original craftsman bungalow on the property.

TWOMEY CELLARS

Twomey Cellars (1183 Dunaweal Ln., Calistoga, 707/942-2489, www.twomey.com, 10am-5pm Mon.-Sat., 11am-5pm Sun., tasting $10) was established by the Duncan family,

the owners of Silver Oak in Oakville and Geyserville who perfected cabernet sauvignon to an art form. By using the same philosophy that informed Silver Oak—exceptional, food-friendly wines—and applying 40 years of winemaking experience, the Duncan family focused on other varietals at their Twomey wineries. Venturing into merlot, pinot noir, and sauvignon blanc, they sourced fruit from California's premier appellations and vineyards and made excellence and sustainability the hallmarks of the Twomey brand. Twomey Calistoga is where their most labor-intensive wine, the Napa Valley merlot is made. Winemaker Daniel Baron crafted this unique merlot through an ancient racking technique known as *soutirage traditionnel,* a slow method of decanting wine that was developed over centuries in Bordeaux. For views of lush, rolling vineyards, visit the tasting room with its elegant curved bar that opens onto a sunny courtyard, and indulge in their approachable, fruit-forward vintages.

STERLING VINEYARDS

When it opened in 1973, this contemporary, monastery-like winery, perched high on a wooded knoll rising straight from the valley floor just south of Calistoga, was hailed as one of the most spectacular wineries in the valley by some—and lambasted by others. **Sterling Vineyards** (1111 Dunaweal Ln., Calistoga, 800/726-6136, www.sterlingvineyards.com, 10:30am-4:30pm Mon.-Fri., 10am-5pm Sat.-Sun., visitor fee $25, under 21 $10, ages 3 and under free) remains one of the most striking to this day, with whitewashed walls and bell towers that look like they're straight from a Greek travel brochure—hard to miss driving north on Highway 29 into Calistoga.

Such an unusual building, with its aerial gondola whisking visitors 300 feet up to the winery, was bound to become a serious tourist attraction, and so it has. At first glance the gondola, ticket booths, and giant parking lot make it feel more like an out-of-season ski resort than a winery, but once at the top of the hill it's all about wine and views.

Once visitors have paid the $25 to get up the

hill, everything is pretty much free, including a fun self-guided tour of the winery on elevated walkways, the views, a sit-down tasting of five wines either inside or out on the patio (weather permitting), and the souvenir wineglass. A large winery, Sterling has more than 1,200 acres of vineyards in just about every Napa appellation, from Los Carneros, from which come some highly rated pinot noir and chardonnay, to high up in the Diamond Mountain appellation, the source of some powerhouse cabernet sauvignon.

It's a unique experience, but involves more walking than at most wineries. Those more interested in the wines than the views should opt for one of the pricier tasting options that include the limited-release and single-vineyard wines for which Sterling is better known ($30-40, which can be put toward a purchase). The only thing sometimes missing is the sort of personal service found at smaller wineries, so you might have to persevere to get any detailed information from the staff about what you're drinking.

CLOS PEGASE

Sterling might be easy to spot perched atop its nearby hill, but just down the road, **Clos Pegase** (1060 Dunaweal Ln., Calistoga, 707/942-4981, www.clospegase.com, 10:30am-5pm daily, tasting $10-30) is truly hard to miss. If the giant pink-and-yellow boxy creation reminds you partly of the whimsical home appliances in your local Target store and partly of a 1980s shopping mall, there's good reason. Clos Pegase was designed in the 1980s by postmodernist architect Michael Graves, better known to most consumers these days as the designer of cheerful teakettles, toasters, and other household paraphernalia.

Graves won a competition sponsored by the San Francisco Museum of Modern Art to design a "temple to wine and art" for entertaining owner Jan Schrem's winemaking passion and for displaying his sizable art collection. The original design, which included a giant statue of the winged horse Pegasus, after which the winery is named, had to be toned down, but

the resulting building, completed in 1987, is still pretty garish against the bucolic backdrop. It could be mistaken for the Napa outpost of a modern art museum; giant sculptures lurk around every corner, and postmodern design touches grace almost every part of the building. It's a place that's a lot easier to admire up close than from afar.

Look for art and sculpture, both ancient and modern, by Kandinsky, Ernst, Moore, and other big names during one of tours offered here at 11:30am and 2pm. Despite the fact that the tour tends to be pitched more toward the less artistically inclined among us, it's really the only way to fully appreciate the winery, its art, and the building's ancient Greek design influences. The tour also takes in the fermentation room and maze of caves burrowed into the hillside behind the winery—nothing particularly notable compared to the arty stuff, but fun nonetheless. Still, the tour doesn't come cheap (adults 21 and over $20, ages 10-20 $10) and includes only two tastings. Reservations are encouraged.

Likewise, the price for tastings are steep, especially when you consider that wine comes secondary here, behind art. But there are some very reasonably priced, approachable pinot noir, merlot, and chardonnay from Carneros behind the counter, as well as a local cabernet sauvignon. There are three tasting options: four estate wines for $20, three reserve wines for $30, and two dessert wines for $10.

CUVAISON

This small winery harkens back to the Napa of decades past. The intimate tasting room at **Cuvaison** (4550 Silverado Trail N., Calistoga, 707/942-6268, www.cuvaison.com, 11am-4pm Fri.-Sat., 10am-5pm Sun.-Thurs., tasting $15-20) doesn't hold busloads of tourists, and the bar might show a few scars, but the tasting room staff know quite a bit about the wine they're pouring and they want to tell you all about it. This isn't a place of snooty wine tasting, but you quickly get the feeling that everyone, regardless of their background, is on even ground and is there to have a good time.

The quaint building sits on the slope of the mountains bordering Napa Valley and shelters several friendly cats. A picnic area invites a longer stop to enjoy the vineyard views with your lunch and a nice bottle of Cuvaison chardonnay, or just to relax and sip one of their light, tasty reds.

CHATEAU MONTELENA

The beautiful French- and Chinese-inspired **Chateau Montelena** (1429 Tubbs Ln., Calistoga, 707/942-5105, www.montelena. com, 9:30am-4pm daily, tasting $20-50) wine estate will forever be remembered for putting Napa Valley on the map when its 1973-vintage chardonnay trounced the best French white burgundies at the famous 1976 Paris tasting.

Today, soft, plush cabernet sauvignon now just as acclaimed as the rich chardonnay at Montelena, and together they account for the bulk of the 35,000-case production. An excellent estate zinfandel is also made, and all are usually available to taste. Cabernet fans can also try a vertical library tasting of the age-worthy but pricey estate cabernet in the intimate stone-walled Estate Room. Reservations for this twice-daily sit-down tasting are essential.

But if the wines aren't enough, the grounds are worth a visit. The stone chateau was built in 1882 by Alfred Tubbs (after whom Tubbs Lane is named), and the ornamental Chinese garden was added in 1965. It is centered around the lush five-acre Jade Lake, crisscrossed with lacquered bridges. For $30 you can take the vineyard tour on Monday and Wednesday at 10:30am, and reservations are not required. For $40 (and a reservation) you can tour the entire estate on Tuesday at 10am, or you can hear the story firsthand of the Judgment of Paris in the Beyond Paris and Hollywood tour that takes place on Thursday at 9:45am. It includes a tasting of the latest vintage of chardonnay and a movie souvenir.

Downtown Tasting Rooms

Like elsewhere in the valley, more small wineries and vintners are getting into the tasting room game. Over the last few years, five have popped up on Lincoln Avenue in the heart of downtown Calistoga.

UP VALLEY VINTNERS

Up Valley Vintners (1371 Lincoln Ave., 707/942-1004, www.upvalleyvintners.com, noon-5pm daily, tasting $10-25) is located down Lincoln Avenue, close to the visitors center. It is the smallest, as it is a co-op, of sorts, of five small wineries in the Calistoga and Diamond Mountain AVAs. The interior is relatively spare and lacks the typical tchotchkes, but the atmosphere is friendly, and it seems there is always a jovial pair chatting up the room's sole pourer. This laid-back vibe is particularly surprising when you consider the high caliber of wine being poured. **Barlow Vineyards** is a small winery producing only 2,000 cases a year from nearly 70 acres off the Silverado Trail. The winery produces some award-winning cabernet and cabernet blends. Farther east at the foot of the Palisades Mountains, the 125-acre **Kenefick Ranch** has been a pioneer in the resurgence of bottling cabernet franc as a stand-alone varietal. Its Bordeaux-style blends are equally celebrated: The flagship Picket Road Red, along with the winery's other single varietals, have frequently earned over 90 points by *Wine Advocate* and *Wine Spectator*. **Zacherle Wines** is the smallest of the bunch, producing only 100-200 cases for each vintage. Unlike the others, you won't find any cabernet, but pinot noir, syrah, riesling, and if you're lucky, a sparkling rosé.

A real standout is the cabernet sauvignon from **Dyer Vineyard.** Made from grapes grown on a 2.3-acre vineyard on Diamond Mountain, Bill and Dawnine Dyer are both veteran winemakers from Sterling and Domaine Chandon, respectively. Their cabernet has a Bordeaux quality and a reputation for excellence, and is difficult to come by, as no more than 400 cases are made a year. Another is **Tofanelli Wines.** Started in 1929, this historic Calistoga winery is dry farmed and produces sophisticated zinfandels, charbono, and petite sirah designed for the dinner table. The Rosé di Carignane is particularly good (especially with a meal) and a great deal at $25. Four flights of four wines are offered, or you can retire with a glass (or two) to the secluded back patio where umbrella-topped tables, brick walls, and climbing vines invite you to stay awhile.

W.H.SMITH

W.H.Smith (1367 Lincoln Ave., 707/942-1194, www.whsmithwines.com, 10am-5pm Sun.-Tues. and Thurs., 10am-6pm Fri.-Sat., tasting $10) is known for cabernets and particularly pinot noirs, many of which are made from grapes grown on the Sonoma Coast. The tasting room also hosts the Wine Sensory Experience, a two-hour class held every day (except Wed.) at 10am. For $45, students learn how to identify different aromas and flavors in wine, as well as how each is cultivated by the winemaker in the first place. It is the only class of its kind in this part of the valley, and the winery keeps it small and intimate with a maximum of only eight students at a time.

RIOS WINE COMPANY AND MALDONADO FAMILY VINEYARDS

Tired of big reds? Step into the parlor-like atmosphere of the joint tasting room of **Rios Wine Company** and **Maldonado Family Vineyards** (1307 Lincoln Ave., 707/942-1376, www.rioswine.com, www.maldonadovineyards.com, 11am-6pm daily, $10). Both ventures are unique as each was started by Mexican immigrants who began their careers working in the vineyards. Today both produce prize-winning wines: The Maldonado chardonnay routinely earns above 90 points from *Wine Spectator,* and the award-winning Rios riesling under the Solovino label.

AUGUST BRIGGS

The crowded tasting room of **August Briggs** (1307 Lincoln Ave., 707/942-4912, www.augustbriggswinery.com, 11am-5pm daily, tasting $5) is a local favorite, perhaps because this small winery produces 16 different wines using seven varietals locally grown in the Napa and Sonoma Valleys—meaning there is something for everyone. For the price of tasting, you'll get five healthy pours. Out of the long menu, be sure to ask for the Old Vine Zinfandel ($35), which is wonderfully full but not too peppery. The Napa Valley "Dijon Clones" pinot noir is another standout, as it is big and bold, especially for the usually shy grape.

VERMEIL WINES

For anyone itching to watch the Niners games while sipping wine, **Vermeil Wines** (1255 Lincoln Ave., 877/668-4334, www.vermeilwines.com, 10am-5:30pm, 10am-8pm Sat.-Sun., free tasting) is the place to go. With a large flat-screen TV, several deep armchairs, and a wall of football memorabilia, this tasting room may resemble a man-cave more than a Napa Valley tasting room. In fact, it is home to hometown boy Dick Vermeil's latest venture. If you can't quite place the name, Vermeil was the NFL coach that took the St. Louis Rams to win the Super Bowl in 2000 and was a popular commentator on CBS and ABC sports. While you might be tempted to think the appropriate beverage here is beer, think again. Vermeil turns out some great wines. The sauvignon blanc has delightful citrus notes, while the cabernet sauvignon and zinfandel have scored above 90 points from *Wine Enthusiast.* The tasting room has two bars, and if you're lucky, one of the winery partners will be on hand to do the pouring.

Wineries by Appointment
LARKMEAD VINEYARDS

Driving up to the farmhouse tasting room of **Larkmead Vineyards** (1100 Larkmead Ln., Calistoga, 707/942-0167, www.larkmead.com, 10am-3pm daily, tasting $40) gives you a sense of what the Napa Valley was like when it was simply farmland that happened to grow grapes. It is modest by Napa Valley standards, a sign that it is more serious about wines than tourists. And this certainly shows in the wines it pours.

Over the years, Larkmead has come to produce very sophisticated wines and won particular praise for its opulent and elegant cabernets made in a classic European style. Anyone wondering just how good the red wines from the

© ELIZABETH LINHART VENEMAN

Vermeil Wines

new Calistoga AVA can be should give these a try.

Just as impressive are the Bordeaux-like blends, including the merlot-dominated Firebelle, a powerfully flavored wine named for the nickname given to Lillie Hitchcock Coit, who christened the Larkmead area back in the 1800s for the preponderance of larks in the area. Also available for tasting is the crisp sauvignon blanc and floral Tocai Friulano. The two flagship wines, Salon and the Solari Reserve, are made in such small quantities that almost the entire production goes to wine club members, a canny move that maintains the exclusivity of Larkmead wines.

Elegant and modern, the tasting room is surrounded by aromatic native plants that are easy to enjoy thanks to the bank of glass doors surrounding the tasting room. Usually open on sunny days, the doors give the tasting room an indoor/outdoor, while the plush chairs and fireplace make it a perfect place to taste wine on one of the valley's gray days. The winery is usually pretty quiet during the week, and that's when it's possible to get a tasting appointment with just a few hours' notice. If you're the only visitors, you might also be treated to a quick tour of the winemaking facilities.

ZAHTILA VINEYARDS

On Highway 29, just as the highway heads over the mountains toward Clear Lake, is a little cluster of modest buildings belonging to this family-owned boutique winery. **Zahtila Vineyards** (2250 Lake County Hwy., Calistoga, 707/942-9251, www.zahtilavineyards.com, 10am-5pm daily, tasting $10) makes some fine cabernet sauvignon and zinfandel. Its relaxed atmosphere and smooth-drinking wines offer a nice change of pace (and price) from the Napa Valley crush. The staff in the cozy tasting room is also a mine of information about other small local wineries. Just don't trip over the chewed toys left lying around by the friendly winery dog.

The specialty here is zinfandel, which is grown in the small Oat Hill Vineyard next to the winery, but also sourced from the Dry

Creek and Russian River Valleys. The cabernet sauvignon comes from the Rutherford and Calistoga areas and goes into the rich, smooth Napa cabernet and flagship Beckstoffer cabernet, which has won many awards and routinely scored above 90 points from *Wine Advocate* and *Wine Enthusiast.*

DIAMOND MOUNTAIN WINERIES

Known to produce big reds with powerful tannins and strong black currant and mineral characteristics, the wineries of Diamond Mountain are worth a visit. Like most mountainside appellations, however, most of the wineries are appointment only. The only exception is the destination winery, Castello di Amorosa, as it sits just off Highway 29.

CASTELLO DI AMOROSA

Driving up to Daryl Sattui's Tuscan wonderland, **Castello di Amorosa** (4045 N. St. Helena Hwy., Calistoga, 707/967-6272, www.castellodiamorosa.com, tours 9:30am-4:30pm Mon.-Fri., 9:30am-5pm Sat.-Sun., general admission ages 21 and over $18, ages 5-20 $8), it is difficult to remember that it is a winery. Everything from the parking attendant who directs you through the large and crowded parking lot to the "general admission" prices screams "Disneyland." And then there is the castle itself: complete with 107 rooms, eight floors, and made from 8,000 tons of stone and 850,000 European bricks. Taking it all in will make anyone want a drink.

Thankfully, the wines are good here. The 38 acres of vineyards planted to cabernet sauvignon, sangiovese, merlot, and primitivo (a relative of zinfandel) around the castle produce intensely flavored red wines typical of Diamond Mountain. They include the excellent-value Il Brigante, a blend of cabernet, merlot, and sangiovese that's a bit like a baby super-Tuscan but with a baby price to go with it. Its big sister is the supple and opulent super-Tuscan blend called La Castellana, named for the traditional lady of the castle. The flagship Diamond Mountain wine is Il Barone, a

powerhouse mountain cabernet. Other reds include well-priced and limited-production sangiovese and merlot. The highlights of the white wines are the Mendocino gewürztraminers, made in both a slightly sweet (dolcino) and bone-dry style. Other whites include several chardonnays, pinot grigio, and a late-harvest semillon. There are also a number of dessert wines and a couple of rosés. General admission includes a tasting of five wines and juice for the kids.

As you would expect, there are many ways to spend more money, from the two-hour tour (adults $33, ages 5-20 $23, no children under 5) to the reserve tasting (general admission plus $10), to the chocolate pairing ($4 extra), to the cheese pairing ($40). Not surprisingly, this is a big destination, particularly for parents eager to make their Wine Country visit palatable to their young children. It is wise to make a reservation on busy weekends.

Wineries by Appointment
◖ SCHRAMSBERG VINEYARDS

If you plan to visit just one of the valley's big champagne makers, the historic **Schramsberg** winery (1400 Schramsberg Rd., via Peterson Dr. off Hwy. 29, Calistoga, 707/942-4558 or 800/877-3623, www.schramsberg.com, 10am-4pm daily, tour and tasting $45) should be high on the list. The winery was established high on the wooded slopes of Diamond Mountain in 1862 by German immigrant Jacob Schram, who had soon made such a name for himself as a maker of high-quality wines that he was paid a visit by a vacationing Robert Louis Stevenson in 1880, a visit memorialized in Stevenson's book *Silverado Squatters.*

The winery was immortalized again in 1972 when its 1969 blanc de blancs was served to President Richard Nixon and China's Premier Zhou Enlai in Beijing for a toast to the normalization of diplomatic relations. In fact, the sales room is full of photos and menus from various White House events at which Schramsberg wines have been served.

Today Schramsberg makes about 45,000 cases of wines, ranging from that historic blanc

A MAGIC KINGDOM OF WINE

© ELIZABETH LINHART VENEMAN

Yes, it really is a castle.

Whether or not you think a replica medieval castle in the Napa Valley is just a bit over the top, it's hard not to be impressed when the fairytale turrets and massive stone walls rear into view as you round a curve on the steep driveway. The product of one man's dream, **Castello di Amorosa** (4045 N. St. Helena Hwy., Calistoga, 707/967-6272, www.castellodiamorosa.com, tours 9:30am-4:30pm Mon.-Fri., 9:30am-5pm

Sat.-Sun., general admission adults $18, ages 5-20 $8) opened in 2007, some 14 years and a reported $30 million after construction began. As its Italian name implies, this castle was a labor of love.

Castello di Amorosa is in many ways no different from other lavish structures built in the valley by eccentric winemakers honoring their family roots or simply realizing grand ambi-

de blancs and a rich, creamy blanc de noirs up to its flagship J. Schram wine, regarded as one of the best California champagnes. The wines are all very complex, thanks to the 67 different vineyards in four California counties from which Schramsberg sources its grapes. To taste them, however, you must sign up for one of the appointment-only tours of the winery, which include a visit to the Victorian mansion, a trip into the spooky bottle-lined caves that date

from the late 1800s, and a lesson on the art of champagne making, all culminating in a sit-down tasting. Each lasts about one hour, 15 minutes and happen daily at 10am, 11:30am, 12:30pm, 1:30pm, and 2:30pm. The price is on the high side, but the setting, the history, and the quality of the wines you taste make it worthwhile.

Even if you cannot book yourself on a tour, it's worth a quick detour from Highway 29 tions. The trend started in the 1880s when the Beringer brothers re-created an ornate Gothic mansion modeled on their German home. Since then, the valley has become host to extravagant buildings inspired by architecture in Greece (Sterling Vineyards), Persia (Darioush), France and Italy (countless wineries), as well as some fascinating modern interpretations of classic structures like Opus One and Clos Pegase. Many of those architectural imposters created quite a stir when first completed, but all have now settled into the valley's cultural and architectural blend. The Castello simply adds a touch more Tuscany to the mix—121,000-square feet of Tuscany, to be precise.

Dario Sattui, a fourth-generation Italian American winemaker and medieval history buff, had already made a name for himself in the valley with the highly successful V. Sattui Winery in St. Helena. His monumental castle is an architectural mash-up, built in just over a decade to resemble the various additions that were commonly made to castles over centuries. It's not based on any particular castle in Tuscany but was inspired by features of many, distilled into a final design by Sattui himself.

Cross the dry moat on the drawbridge, enter through the iron gates into the stone passageway, and sign up for the two-hour **tour and tasting** (adults $33, ages 5-20 $23, no children under 5). The basic wine-tasting tour (included in the general admission) barely hints at the his-tory in the towers rising four stories above and passageways that plunge four stories below. First stop on the tour is the Great Hall, a two-story marvel of frescoes, coffered ceilings, and stone walls fit for any wine-fueled banquet. The cloistered main courtyard beyond, with its tiny chapel and colorful planters, could be out of any ancient French or Italian village. The towers offer strategic views over the valley and even have chutes to pour hot oil on the advancing hordes below.

The best parts of the castle lie underground. A warren of cool, damp passageways descend to catacombs and vaulted cellars, including the breathtaking, 130-foot-long barrel room with its vast cross-vaulted ceiling. There's even a dungeon stocked with some particularly heinous torture instruments—including an original iron maiden, which is lined with spikes to impale hapless victims inside. Next door is an aptly named "pit of despair," into which victims were thrown to starve to death.

Everything was painstakingly re-created using traditional materials and a small army of artisans. Every piece of iron, from the elaborate gates and dragon-head sconces down to the nails in the massive wooden doors, was hand-forged in Italy, where the antique bricks and tiles were also sourced. Much of the stone used in the walls was quarried locally, and the pieces were hand-shaped on-site to fit together like a giant three-dimensional jigsaw.

up the perilously narrow wooded road (with almost invisible speed bumps) just to see the mansion and the ornate gardens that are like a Victorian oasis hidden in the forest. You can also buy any of the wines and look at the old photos in the sales room, which is open all day.

REVERIE VINEYARD & WINERY
Located at the end of the long driveway off Diamond Mountain Road, **Reverie Winery** (1520 Diamond Mountain Rd., Calistoga, 707/942-6800 or 800/738-3743, www.reveriewine.com, by appointment only, availability depends on the time of year) shares a hidden sun-drenched valley surrounded by terraced vineyards that are key to its success as well as the success of the neighboring wineries that share this little part of wine-growing heaven. It is one of the few wineries that produces exclusively estate wine.

This is even more impressive because it grows nine varietals on its 40 acres. All are red, with the exception of the roussanne, and made in the restrained French tradition of low alcohol, food-friendly wines. Big and ripe with muscular tannins, the reds are classic Diamond Mountain wines, enhanced (at least mentally) by the alfresco tasting experience under towering redwood trees.

Part of the tasting is a relaxed but educational walk through the property, which includes the winery, caves, and redwood grove. Along the way, different wines are tasted, and it is unlikely that your glass will ever be empty.

VON STRASSER WINERY
The drive off Diamond Mountain Road first passes the unobtrusive home of the **Von Strasser Winery** (1510 Diamond Mountain Rd., Calistoga, 707/942-0930, www.vonstrasser.com, 10:30am-4:30pm daily, tour and tasting $20), established in 1990 by Rudy von Strasser, who was instrumental in putting Diamond Mountain on the wine map. He spearheaded the alliance of local growers that finally succeeded in having Diamond Mountain declared its own sub-appellation within Napa Valley in 2001, after almost a decade of trying.

The Estate Vineyard cabernet is the wine that Von Strasser is probably best known for, balancing powerful tannins with equally powerful fruit, resulting in high ratings from critics almost every year. This and a couple of other cabernets are usually available to taste by appointment as part of a flight of five wines at the low-key tasting room. For an additional $10 you can enjoy your wine with artisan chocolate while touring the winery's cave, or for another $20, sit down in the cave's library for a selection of cheese paired to your flight. All guests are welcome to picnic on the property at the conclusion of their tour and tasting.

SIGHTS
◖ Sharpsteen Museum of Calistoga History
The quirky little **Sharpsteen Museum** (1311 Washington St., Calistoga, 707/942-5911, www.sharpsteen-museum.org, 11am-4pm daily, $3 donation requested) was donated to the city in the 1970s by its creators, Ben and Bernice Sharpsteen, and depicts up-valley life from the days of the Wappo people to the early 1900s. Its main claim to fame is a beautifully painted diorama depicting Calistoga in its hot springs heyday, but it also has some more traditional exhibits, many no doubt enhanced by the skills of Ben Sharpsteen, who was an Academy Award-winning animator.

Next door is one of the frilly little cottages built by Sam Brannan in the 1860s for his groundbreaking Hot Springs Resort in Calistoga. It was moved here in the 1970s, leaving only one of Brannan's cottages where it was built—at the Brannan Cottage Inn on Wappo Avenue.

Old Faithful Geyser
Although it may not really be worth the time or money, visitors continue to flock to Calistoga's **Old Faithful Geyser** (1299 Tubbs Ln., Calistoga, 707/942-6463, www.oldfaithfulgeyser.com, 9am-6pm daily spring-fall, 9am-5pm daily winter, adults $10, children 6-12 $3, under 6 free), one of only three geysers in the world reliable enough to get the "Old Faithful" moniker. There must be something hypnotic about the thought of watching water shoot 60 feet or more into the air that keeps people coming. Or perhaps it's the free mud bath into which you can unwittingly sink if you get too close to the edge of the pools. Or maybe it's the allure of the 1960s era roadside attraction. Just hope you don't get there right after an eruption has finished, or it could be as long as a 45-minute wait until the next one (the gap between eruptions varies depending on the season, so check the website for the latest updates). Still, that's time enough to open your faithful old wallet for some overpriced and tacky Old Faithful gifts. Even the famous fainting goats near the entrance seem bored by all the fuss and rarely faint on cue, as their "genetic defect" is supposed to guarantee. There are also

© ELIZABETH LINHART VENEMAN

Calistoga's Old Faithful Geyser is a popular roadside attraction.

a few sheep and llamas at the little petting zoo to keep the goats company. A coin-op feeder lets visitors feed and pet the animals—a perfect means of inspiring patience in children who may grow tired of waiting for the geyser to erupt.

Petrified Forest

A natural attraction that illustrates the area's volcanic past but with far more scenic value than Old Faithful (though no goats) is the **Petrified Forest** (4100 Petrified Forest Rd., 707/942-6667, www.petrifiedforest.org, 9am-7pm daily summer, 9am-5pm daily winter, adults $6, seniors/juniors $5, children $3), a couple of miles west of Calistoga on the road to Santa Rosa. Like Old Faithful Geyser down the hill, the experience feels very homespun with little in the way of glossy corporate tourist facilities. You also might start wondering what you paid for, because the short trails meander through what seem like recently fallen red-wood trees. In fact, they were long ago turned to stone at such a microscopic level that they

still look almost like real wood rather than the fossils they are. In the distance looms Mount St. Helena, believed to have been the source of the volcanic eruption that buried the trees millions of years ago and started the long petrification process. To learn more about it and the flora and fauna of the area, join the Meadow Hike, a guided tour available on weekends at 11am. The price (adults $16, children 12-17 $15, under 12 free) includes admission. You can also learn more about the forest by browsing the lovely little visitors center and gift shop. There are lots of rocks and minerals, earthy handcrafted gifts, books on geology, and a few rare shards of the petrified trees from this very forest.

Pioneer Cemetery

Looking for your Napa ancestors? Just like prowling through historic graveyards? Stop at the Napa Valley **Pioneer Cemetery** (Bothe-Napa Valley State Park, 3801 St. Helena Hwy. N., Calistoga, 707/942-4575, www.parks. ca.gov, sunrise-sunset, $8 day-use fee). Here you'll find the graves of many of Napa's earliest settlers and some of the more prominent early families. The cemetery seems to undergo regular maintenance, since paths between plots are kept clear and walkable. But many of the graves are overgrown with vines—some even have full-sized oak trees growing through them. The whole area is covered by a dense canopy of forest foliage, making it a pleasantly cool place to visit on hot summer days. You can explore up the hillside, where the paths get more overgrown and some of the tombstones are still old wooden planks, their lettering worn away. If you're interested in genealogy, start at the front entrance of the cemetery, where a map and alphabetical survey of the cemetery are posted. One warning about visiting this cemetery: No, not ghosts—lack of parking. There's enough room at the front for one small car. Otherwise, you'll need to park elsewhere and walk carefully along and across Highway 29 to the gate.

Pope Valley

Sleepy **Pope Valley** is the unlikely setting for California Historic Landmark No. 939. Even more unlikely is that California would designate a collection of thousands of hubcaps strung from posts, fences, and trees as a historic landmark. But such is the importance of this strange collection to the state's eclectic folk-art scene (or so someone thought) that the **Hubcap Ranch,** created by Emanuel "Litto" Damonte from the 1950s to his death in 1985, was given its lofty status, and Litto was immortalized as the Pope Valley Hubcap King.

It is still a private ranch, so don't expect any Wine Country-style tours, though you're welcome to leave a hubcap from the rental car or your own to ensure the collection keeps growing. The ranch's dogs seem to love trying to scare visitors, so don't be surprised when they hurl their snarling bodies at the fence behind the landmark plaque.

Litto's grandson, Mike Damonte, has kept up the folk-art tradition that his grandfather inadvertently started when he hung lost hubcaps on his fence in case their hapless owners wanted them back. The growing collection proved to be a magnet, and soon neighbors and anonymous visitors were leaving hubcaps rather than taking them. Now, half a century later, there are, it is said, about 5,000 of the things glinting in the sun, from lavish chrome 1960s trim to the present-day plastic wannabes.

Hubcap Ranch is easy to get to and easy to spot. From the Silverado Trail, head up Deer Park Road, through the small college town of Angwin, and down through the forest to the auto-repair shop, junkyard, and general store that constitute downtown Pope Valley. At that intersection, turn left onto Pope Valley Road. Hubcap Ranch is about two miles farther, at 6654 Pope Valley Road just past the Pope Valley Winery, though you certainly won't need to look for the number on a mailbox.

While you're in the area, the **Pope Valley Winery** (6613 Pope Valley Rd., 707/965-1246, www.popevalleywinery.com, 11am-5pm Thurs.-Sun., call ahead Mon.-Tues., free tasting) is worth a stop, despite its sprawling, scrappy-looking setting. The original three-story winery building was built in 1909 and operated as the Sam Haus Winery until 1959. Since then a variety of owners have tried to make a go of it in this remote location, the latest being a group of valley residents who bought the old buildings in 1998 and now make about 4,000 cases of mainly red wines from the 80 acres of Pope Valley vineyards, including zinfandel, cabernet sauvignon, and sangiovese.

ENTERTAINMENT

For the sleepiest and most mellow town in the Napa Valley, Calistoga has some of the best nightlife. This is still Wine Country, however, so don't expect too much beyond live local bands and the ability to buy a beer after 11pm. The **Hydro Bar & Grill** (1403 Lincoln Ave., 707/942-9777) sometimes hosts local live music on weekend nights, and the **Napa Valley Brewing Company** at the Calistoga Inn (1250 Lincoln Ave., 707/942-4101, www.calistogainn.com) offers live jazz or blues every night of the week on the creek-side patio during the summer and often on weekends in the winter. There's also a popular open-mike night on

Wednesday and themed music on most other weekday nights hosted by the house DJ. More information is available online or by phone from the Calistoga Inn.

In Calistoga, the "M" in March stands for **Mustard, Mud, and Music Festival** (707/942-6333, www.calistogavisitors.com). The second weekend in March, Calistoga celebrates spring with a multitude of eating, drinking, and musical events. Some of the spas have specials (it is a mud festival, after all), while jazz plays noon-6pm in the downtown Wine Pavilion on Washington Street, and then on into the night at various bars and restaurants. Tickets are $40 and include 10 food- or wine-tasting coupons as well as a souvenir wineglass.

However, Calistoga puts its best party hat on for the **Napa County Fair** (1435 N. Oak St., Calistoga, 707/942-5111, www.napacountyfair.org, adults $10, children 7-12 $5, under 6 free) held every July 4th weekend at the Napa County Fairgrounds. The parade through town, countless live music events, a plethora

© ELIZABETH LINHART VENEMAN

There are many fine items in Calistoga's shops.

of gourmet food on sticks, carnival rides for the kids, and more (and better) wine than at most county fairs is small-town Americana at its best. Even the most cynical will be filled with patriotic pride at this fun, unpretentious annual event.

SHOPPING

Like many things in Calistoga, shopping is a little more down-to-earth here than elsewhere in the valley. Sure, there are plenty of gift shops, but there's a decidedly artisanal feel to most of them, like the **American Indian Trading Company** (1407 Lincoln Ave., Calistoga, 707/942-9330, www.aitcoc.com, 10am-6pm daily), which sells arts, crafts, and jewelry from Native American tribes all over the country, including a few local groups. On Highway 29 just south of Lincoln Avenue is **Calistoga Pottery** (1001 Foothill Blvd., Calistoga, 707/942-0216, 9am-5pm Mon.-Sat., 11am-5pm Sun.), another good place to buy something original from local artists who have supplied some of the valley's biggest wineries and restaurants with their stoneware. And, of course, you can taste olive oil here, too, at the new **Calistoga Olive Oil Company** (1441 Lincoln Ave., Calistoga, 707/942-1329, http://calistogaoliveoilcompany.com, 10am-5pm daily), which not only produces its own label of local olive oil but has a dizzying array of infused salts.

But unlike other valley towns, in Calistoga you'll find a string of secondhand and consignment stores when you first turn into town off Highway 29. The quality of clothes and household goods found here is exceptional. For example, don't be surprised if you see a mink stole outside **Sugardaddy's** (1333 Lincoln Ave., Calistoga, 707/942-1600, 10am-5pm Mon.-Fri., 10am-4pm Sun.) Inside there is everything from a $10 trashcan to a $250 set of silver. You can also find fondue pots, bamboo cutting boards, used DVDs, a ton of hats, and great deals on women's clothing.

Not to be left out, **A Man's Supply** (1343 Lincoln Ave., 707/942-2280, www.amanssupply.com, 10am-6pm daily) satisfies the needs of the Y chromosome with plenty of work clothes, outdoor gear, watches, pocket knives, and boots. And everyone will find something to pique their interest at **Copperfields Books** (1330 Lincoln Ave., Calistoga, 707/942-1616, http://copperfieldsbooks.com, 10am-7pm daily). This general-interest bookstore has a great selection of current fiction as well as the kind of cooking section you would expect in Wine Country.

At the eastern end of Lincoln Avenue is the historic **Calistoga Depot** (1458 Lincoln Ave., Calistoga), the second-oldest remaining railroad depot in the country, built by Sam Brannan in 1868 and crucial to the early success of Calistoga's Victorian spas. It is now home to a handful of funky little stores, some of them in six old railroad cars parked on the tracks that lead to nowhere. **Calistoga Wine Stop** (707/942-5556, http://calistogawinestop. net, 10am-6pm daily) is in the main depot building and has a great selection of wines from both Napa and Sonoma. Most are from smaller producers (usually 3,000 cases or less) that are hard to find elsewhere. Each day a red and a white are available for tasting.

Wine aficionados will also probably enjoy sniffing around the small **Enoteca Wine Shop** (1348 Lincoln Ave., Calistoga, 707/942-1117, 11:30am-5:30pm daily), which specializes in smaller (sometimes cult) producers of wines from California and beyond. Another fascinating wine shop, one that prides itself on selling hard-to-find boutique California wines, is the **Wine Garage** (1020 Foothill Blvd., Calistoga, 707/942-5332, 11am-6:30pm Mon.-Sat., 11am-4:30pm Sun.) on Foothill Boulevard just south of Lincoln Avenue. Owner Todd Miller travels throughout the lesser-known wine regions of Northern California trying and buying wines from small wineries, loading them onto his truck, and bringing them back to the shop. No bottle costs more than $25, and many are under $15—a refreshing change in a valley of big wine names and big prices.

RECREATION
Calistoga Spas
During his stay here in 1880, Robert Louis Stevenson observed that Calistoga "seems to repose on a mere film above a boiling, subterranean lake." That mineral-laden boiling water fueled the growth of one of the biggest spa destinations in California. Railroad baron Samuel Brannan first cashed in on the endless hot water supply in 1862 with his Hot Springs Resort, and by the late 1860s the new railroad was bringing the fashionable and well-heeled from San Francisco to immerse themselves.

The emphasis of the dozens of spas these days has broadened to include everything from restorative volcanic mud to mineral soaks, wraps, and facials. The clientele has also broadened to include the less well-heeled, drawn by the straightforward, no-nonsense spa treatments here that dispense with the more luxurious frills offered by the bigger Napa Valley and Sonoma super-resorts. Don't go expecting glamorous establishments straight out of a glossy magazine spread—some of the places look like decidedly unglamorous motels in need of some restorative work themselves.

The region's Wappo people were the first to discover the unlikely pleasure of soaking in the local mud (one wonders who first had the idea and why). These days the mud is usually a mixture of dark volcanic ash, peat (for buoyancy), and hot mineral water that suspends your body, relaxes muscles, and draws out impurities in the skin, all accompanied by a rather off-putting sulfurous smell. A 10-15-minute soak is usually followed by a rinse in crystal-clear mineral water and a steam wrap with or without piped music. Aromatherapies, massages, and other hedonistic treatments can be added afterward but will quickly run up the price. Those worried about lying in someone else's impurities can take comfort from the claims that the mud is regularly flushed with fresh spring water. There is evidently such a thing as "clean" mud.

Wherever and whatever the treatment, remember that the heat can rapidly dehydrate your body, so lay off the wine beforehand and don't plan to hike to the top of Mount St. Helena afterward. Reservations are usually needed, but you might luck out just by walking in, especially midweek. Most spas are also open late, making them an ideal way to wrap up a long day of touring (pun intended).

On the site of Brannan's original resort is the **Indian Springs Resort** (1712 Lincoln Ave., Calistoga, 707/942-4913, www.indianspringscalistoga.com, 9am-8pm daily), which specializes in 100 percent volcanic mud bath treatments ($85), using the volcanic ash from its 16 acres of land, and mineral baths ($70). It also has what is said to be California's oldest continuously operating swimming pool, an Olympic-sized version built in 1913 and fed by warm spring water. In fact, you can usually see the puffs of steam from the natural hot springs on-site. Spa customers can lounge by the pool as long as they want, though it can get crowded, and the water is a little too warm for any serious swimming.

Another muddy Calistoga institution announced by its big, red neon sign is the funky **Dr. Wilkinson's Hot Springs** (1507 Lincoln Ave., Calistoga, 707/942-4102, www.drwilkinson.com, 8:30am-5:30pm daily), founded by an eccentric chiropractor in the 1950s who developed his own secret recipe for the mud, which his children still guard closely today. "The Works," a 1.5-hour pampering with mud bath, facial, mineral soak, and blanket wrap, costs $89. For $50 more, you can finish with a 30-minute massage, and there are plenty of other competitively priced packages available.

At the **Calistoga Hot Springs Spa** (1006 Washington St., Calistoga, 707/942-6269, www.calistogaspa.com, 8:30am-4:30pm Tues.-Thurs., 8:30am-9pm Fri.-Mon.), you can indulge in a mud bath, mineral bath, or all the usual spa treatments, but what stands out here is access to Calistoga Hot Springs' four outdoor mineral pools. The lap pool is the coolest at 80°F and set up for serious swimmers. The 90°F wading pool with fountains offers fun health benefits for the whole family. Another large soaking pool is set to 100°F and meant primarily for adults. Finally, the enormous 104°F octagonal jetted spa sits under a gazebo—the perfect location to relax and enjoy the serenity of spa country.

The **Lincoln Avenue Spa** (1339 Lincoln Ave., Calistoga, 707/942-2950, www.lincolnavenuespa.com, 10am-6pm Sun.-Thurs., 10am-7pm Fri.-Sat.) offers couples the chance to float in twin tubs of mud in a private room ($149). There is a choice of four types of mud, including an Ayurvedic herbal mud and an antioxidant-laden wine mud containing wine, grape seed oil, and green tea. It also offers salt scrubs, with or without accompanying mud, and a full range of massages and facials. No jokes about spa treatments breaking the bank here—this spa is in an impregnable-looking stone building that was a Victorian-era bank.

At the **Lavender Hill Spa** (1015 Foothill Blvd., Calistoga, 707/942-4495, www.lavenderhillspa.com, 9am-9pm Thurs.-Mon., 9am-7pm Tues.-Wed.) the mud is used only once before being discarded and is an international affair, containing Calistoga volcanic ash, French sea kelp, Dead Sea salt, and the trademark lavender oil. Like most treatments here, the mud bath ($89) is available for singles or couples. For the same price there is also a Thai milk bath with sea kelp and some fruity essential oils that is part of a whole range of other Thai-inspired massages and facials, all in a relaxing garden-like setting.

There is an equally diverse selection of ways to immerse yourself at **Mount View Spa** (1457 Lincoln Ave., Calistoga, 707/942-5789 or 800/816-6877, www.mountviewhotel.com, 9am-9pm daily) in the namesake hotel, including mineral mud baths, aromatherapy baths and saunas, mud and seaweed wraps, massages, and facial treatments in perhaps the classiest setting in Calistoga. The mineral mud baths ($70, couples $80) and wraps might contain grape seeds, aromatherapy essences, as well as Moor mud added to the water. Massages start at $75 for 25 minutes, and the huge selection culminates with a three-hour $360 extravaganza called the Head to Toe package, which includes a mineral bath, body polish, Swedish massage, and facial. The hotel's pool can also be used by spa customers.

LEAVE WINE (AND CLOTHES) BEHIND

Put away the camera, forget about wineries, leave your cynicism behind, and take off all your clothes (if you want to) at the historic and decidedly alternative **Harbin Hot Springs** (Harbin Springs Rd., off Big Canyon Rd., Middletown, 707/987-2477 or 800/622-2477, www.harbin.org), about a half hour north of Calistoga beyond Mount St. Helena in rural Lake County.

In some sense, this place could be described as a hot springs resort. It has the natural springs and the history of its Calistoga spa cousins to the south, dating from the late 1800s when the sick and infirm sought out the natural waters here. A more accurate description these days, however, would be a New Age eco-resort still running on 1960s flower power. It's a place where you're far more likely to hear about the joy of finding a higher state of consciousness than the joy of savoring the best cabernet in Napa. That's if you hear anything. In some parts of the resort, even a whisper will elicit gentle but firm rebukes that might conjure up fears of some bizarre karmic retribution. It also has a bit of a reputation for being a pickup joint, both gay and straight, which makes you wonder how one hooks up in silence.

Nevertheless, there's enough on offer within the 1,200 acres to please even a wine-soaked cynic—from hiking trails in the hills to the series of indoor-outdoor hot and cold pools among the trees; from the organic food store to the communal kitchen. Best of all is the endless flow of free classes and workshops ranging from dance and yoga to meditation and massage. Harbin is perhaps best known for its Watsu massage—a form of Shiatsu massage performed while you float in a pool.

Nearly all the activities are free after paying a day-use fee of $30 (weekdays) or $40 (weekends), though at least one person in your party will need to buy a $10 trial membership to the nonprofit organization that runs Harbin. If you only want to sunbathe naked (or clothed) for half a day or take a yoga class, the six-hour fee is $10 less. Check the website for a full schedule of events and classes.

Another reason to come here is for the wide range of accommodations. They range from dorm rooms ($40-60, bring your own towels and bedding) and basic rooms with shared baths ($60-95) up to rooms with half baths (from $130 midweek, $190 weekends) and three cottages tucked away in the woods ($170-190 midweek). Three cottages sit near the pool area (as of this printing more are in the process of being built farther away on the meadow) and cost $170-260, and tent cabins sit interspersed among the campsites and go for $80-100. The most bizarre rooms are in a space-age domed complex perched on a hillside that look as though they were designed by an architect on acid. The double rooms with wacky windows and shared bathrooms cost $100-190. Camping in the meadows is also an option and is free with the day-use fee ($30-40), though no fires or camping stoves are allowed, so you'll be eating in one of the on-site vegetarian restaurants or using the communal kitchen.

Robert Louis Stevenson State Park

By far the best views in the valley, and perhaps the entire Wine Country, are from the top of Napa's highest peak, Mount St. Helena, which is at the northern end of the valley in this park (Hwy. 29, Calistoga, 707/942-4575, www.parks.ca.gov, open sunrise-sunset, free) named for the mountain's most famous Victorian visitor.

Stevenson honeymooned in a cabin here after traveling from his native Scotland to marry Fanny Osbourne, the woman he met at an artists' retreat. The area had just been abandoned by silver miners following the rapid rise and fall of the **Silverado mine** in the 1870s, after which the Silverado Trail and Stevenson's account of his brief stay in the valley, *Silverado Squatters,* is named.

The happy couple's cabin is long gone, marked only by a small monument partway up the five-mile trail to the summit. Look out for two big dirt parking lots on either side of the road about eight miles north of Calistoga on Highway 29. The **Mount St. Helena Trail** starts from the western lot and has virtually no shade, together with some particularly steep sections—it climbs about 2,000 feet in five miles to the 4,339-foot summit of the mountain—so hiking it in the middle of a hot summer day is not recommended. On the clearest days, usually in spring, the 360-degree views stretch for nearly 200 miles, and sometimes you can even see San Francisco's skyline or Mount Shasta far to the north. In winter there is often a dusting of snow near the peak. Those not so determined to get to the summit can take a spur off the main trail at about the 3.5-mile point to the 4,000-foot South Peak, which has impressive views of the valley.

East from the parking lot is the start of the **Table Rock Trail,** a shorter and less strenuous 2.2-mile trail that climbs out of the woodland and past volcanic rock outcroppings to a ridge overlooking the flat moonscape known as Table Rock and the entire valley to the south. The more adventurous can connect to the **Palisades Trail,** which crosses Table Rock and eventually meets the historic Oat Hill Mine Road leading down into the valley, though that turns the hike into a daylong expedition and ends miles from the parking lot.

Hiking

If you want to stretch your legs, the 8.25-mile **Oat Hill Mine Trail** departs from a trailhead (street parking only) at the intersection of Highway 29 and the Silverado Trail. It winds up 2,000 feet above the valley through volcanic formations, groves of Douglas fir, gray pine, and cypress as well as chaparral and grassland, which is known to yield an exceptional bounty of wildflowers. The trail was constructed in 1893 for access to nearby quicksilver mines. You can still see the ruts carved by heavy wagons in the soft volcanic rock. Midway, there are ruins of the Holmes homestead settled in 1893. You'll see many locals on the trail, and it crosses parkland as

well as private property. Unfortunately, there is no loop, but the views and backcountry setting are worth the up and back trek. The trail is open to hikers, mountain bikers, horseback riders, and unleashed (but still within voice command) dogs.

Golf

Like elsewhere in the valley, there is plenty to lure visitors out of the tasting room. The Napa County Fairgrounds in the heart of Calistoga has its own nine-hole golf course. The **Mt. St. Helena Golf Course** (2025 Grant St., Calistoga, 707/942-9966, www.mtsthelenagolfcourse.org, 7am-dusk daily; $12-20 Mon.-Fri., $14-26 Sat.-Sun.) is charming and inexpensive—perfect for any player. For those younger or less experienced, it is flat and straight, with easier lines than some other courses, while intermediate-level players will appreciate the challenge of the trees along the fairways.

ACCOMMODATIONS

Calistoga is one of the cheapest places in the valley for most purchases, from food and gas to a place to stay. This is still Wine Country, however, so "cheap" is a relative term, and prices have risen faster than the valley average in the past few years. Calistoga might finally be cashing in on its charms.

Some of the Victorian B&Bs strung along Highway 29 and Foothill Boulevard seem downright reasonable during the week, but rates can almost double on summer weekends, much like everywhere else in the valley. The best bargains are probably the numerous spa resorts that offer slightly less elegant motel-style rooms for slightly more reasonable prices. All generally offer free continental breakfast, though with some you might be left wondering which continent manages to function on such meager morning sustenance.

Whatever the accommodation, remember that this end of the valley is the hottest, and sleeping without air-conditioning in the height of summer can be a challenge. As in the rest of the valley, there is also a penalty to pay for wanting to stay during a weekend, when a two-night minimum is pretty standard. And that's if you can find a room. As always, book plenty of time in advance July-October.

Under $150

To use the term "bargain" to describe the **Calistoga Inn** (1250 Lincoln Ave., Calistoga, 707/942-4101, www.calistogainn.com, $80-120) gives guests an old-school hotel experience, complete with shared bathrooms and showers (but with sinks in each room). The inn, in continuous operation for over 100 years, offers a continental breakfast each morning, an English pub downstairs that serves lunch and dinner, and perhaps the best bargain rooms in the whole of Napa Valley. Each of the 18 guest rooms provides a small, cozy haven with a queen bed, simple but charming furnishings, and a view of the town. Be sure to make reservations in advance—at these prices, rooms go quickly, especially in summer and fall! And be aware that the pub downstairs has live music acts four nights a week, so the party can get loud (and fun!) on weekends. Unfortunately, the party has been on hiatus. In late August 2012, a fire broke out, causing the historic inn to do some extensive upgrading. As of this printing, the word is that the inn will remain charming and inexpensive, and reopen in May 2013.

A more rustic accommodation option is at the **Mountain Home Ranch** (3400 Mountain Home Ranch Rd., off Petrified Forest Rd., Calistoga, 707/942-6616, www.mountainhomeranch.com, $70-145), up in the hills about a 10-minute drive from Calistoga. This is a down-home family B&B and working ranch with rooms in the main house and separate cottages that are more practical than stylish. They are fairly cheap and private but a little rundown and by no means luxurious. Part of the charm of the ranch, however, is its peaceful rural setting. Hiking trails lead from the accommodations to the farm and down to a creek—just be sure to get directions because the trail is not obvious. It's a great place for outdoorsy types who don't want the hassles of camping and for families with adventurous kids who will enjoy two swimming pools, a lake, volleyball and tennis courts, table-tennis tables, a basketball hoop, plus a coterie of barnyard animals. Parents might equally enjoy the no-fuss meal options in the main house.

$150-250

This is the price range into which many of Calistoga's spas and B&Bs fall. One of the best values is the Calistoga institution **Dr. Wilkinson's Hot Springs Resort** (1507 Lincoln Ave., Calistoga, 707/942-4102, www.drwilkinson.com, $149-300). Best known for its mud baths, the doctor also has 42 basic rooms just a few steps from all the shops and restaurants of Lincoln Avenue. From the outside this looks like a 1950s motel, but the rooms have a little more going for them, with modern and tasteful (if slightly sparse) furnishings, including comfortable beds, air-conditioning, and fairly standard motel levels of equipment. Don't expect luxury at this price, although the charm of the lively resort more than compensates. The cheapest rooms are arranged around the courtyard or pool, while for a bit more you can get a lot more charm at one of the rooms in the small neighboring Victorian cottage houses, though there's little in the way of additional creature comforts to justify the higher prices.

Equally old school is the **Hideaway Cottages** (1412 Fair Way, Calistoga, 707/942-4108, www.hideawaycottages.com, $164-305). This collection of 1940s-era bungalows is primly decorated in cream colors and the occasional plaid bedspread. They also retain their original details like scallop-edged kitchen cupboards, tile countertops, and charming built-in glass cabinets. Many of the cottages have sitting rooms, full kitchens, and outside sitting areas. All are painted a crisp white with a country-blue trim, and all face the communal leafy grounds where lawns offer plenty of spots to lounge around the pool and hot tub. In the interest of quiet, no pets or children under 18 are allowed.

Another inexpensive bungalow style option is the **EuroSpa and Inn** (1202 Pine St., Calistoga, 707/942-6829, www.eurospa.com, $225), a motel-style establishment on a peaceful residential street just a block from Lincoln Avenue. Rooms in the small bungalows arranged around a central parking lot are fairly tastefully furnished and come with a long list of standard features including whirlpool tubs, air-conditioning, gas fireplaces (certainly not needed in summer), Internet access, and refrigerators. Being on the edge of town, the inn's pool looks onto vineyards and is where the continental breakfast is usually served in summer. Winter rates drop nearly 50 percent, but unfortunately it is too chilly to take advantage of the pool and outside lounge.

Staying in a little piece of history is cheaper than you might think at the **Brannan Cottage Inn** (109 Wapoo Ave., Calistoga, 707/942-4200, www.brannancottageinn.com, $235). The Victorian cottage with its white picket fence is the only cottage from Sam Brannan's original Calistoga resort that still stands where it was built, on a quiet street just off Calistoga's main drag. It is now on the National Register of Historic Places and contains six rooms furnished in tasteful and restrained Victorian style, all with air-conditioning, private bathrooms, views of the pretty gardens, and a private entrance from the wraparound porch. The prices may seem steep for the cozy rooms, but keep in mind that $30 comes off the price per night in winter. The owners recently adopted a Jack Russell puppy, Pinot Grigio, as the inn's official mascot, so be prepared to be jumped on and loved to death. Aside from the refreshing touch of chaos that an energetic canine brings, it also means that the inn is now open to all well-behaved four-footed guests.

One of the biggest old buildings in downtown Calistoga (though that's not saying much) is home to the **Mount View Hotel** (1457 Lincoln Ave., Calistoga, 707/942-6877 or 800/816-6877, www.mountviewhotel.com, $264), which brings a bit of urban style within walking distance of almost everything Calistoga has to offer. The cheapest queen and king rooms can be a bit on the small side, but all 29 rooms and suites have a slightly eclectic mix of modern furnishings with Victorian

antique and art deco touches harking back to the hotel's 1920s and 1930s heyday. The list of standard features is impressive for Calistoga and stretches to CD players in some rooms and free wireless Internet access. The more expensive suites have claw-foot tubs and wet bars, and the pricier suites have balconies overlooking the street. Best of all are the three separate cottages, each with its own small outdoor redwood deck and hot tub.

If you're able to get a reservation for one of the four rooms at the **Hotel d'Amici** (1436 Lincoln Ave., Calistoga, 707/942-1007, www.hoteldamici.com, $200), consider yourself lucky. The charming hotel in the center of downtown offers spacious and comfortable junior suites in the heart of Calistoga for very reasonable rates, which makes it very popular. The two smaller suites at the back of the hotel are the cheapest, while the larger suites at the front of the building have fireplaces and share a balcony looking over Lincoln Avenue. All the rooms are decorated in a simple, clean style and offer private bathrooms with soaking tubs, down comforters, cable television, and a bottle of Rutherford Grove wine (the Pestoni family owns both the winery and the hotel). A continental breakfast appears as if by magic outside the door every morning, but the lack of on-site staff can make late-night arrivals challenging. Be sure to keep the confirmation letter for the code to get into the hotel.

Hats off to the owners of **The Pink Mansion** (1415 Foothill Blvd., Calistoga, 707/942-0558 or 800/238-7465, www.pinkmansion.com, $250) for not even attempting to come up with a clever name for their bright pink Victorian, which dates from 1875. The honest name is matched by some unique features that were added by the last person to live there full-time, the eclectic Alma Simic—like the small heated pool in what looks like a Victorian parlor. She's the one who painted the house pink in the 1930s, the color it has been ever since. The woodsy surroundings, quaint but not overly frilly furnishings, and features like claw-foot tubs and air-conditioning make this one of the pricier establishments along this stretch of road, however. The smallest rooms have no shortage of charm, but the gargantuan and luxurious Master Suite, dripping with period features and exotic woods, includes a wood-burning fireplace, marble bath for two, and a separate sitting room and deck.

Over $250

One of the prettiest spa resorts in Calistoga with among the most tastefully decorated rooms and a giant spring-fed pool is **Indian Springs** (1712 Lincoln Ave., Calistoga, 707/942-4913, www.indianspringscalistoga.com, $250-300). The cheapest rooms are in the two-story mission-style lodge building, which used to be a neighboring hotel but was bought and renovated by Indian Springs in 2005. The 1940s-era cottages that the resort is best known for are on the pricey side, but are made more palatable by the plank flooring, kitchenettes, and barbecues on their back porches. At one end of the spectrum are Sam's Bungalows, named for Sam Brannan, who set up his Victorian-era resort on the land that Indian Springs now occupies. They start at $285 during the summer (July-Oct.) and on winter weekends but are only $195 midweek in winter. The palm-lined driveway is surrounded by the cozy one- and two-bedroom Palm Row cottages that start at $410 during the summer ($215 midweek in winter) and are probably the best bargains with their separate sitting area with a sofa bed. Ask for numbers 16 or 17—they back onto open fields for some extra isolation. Both the Sam's and Palm Row bungalows share front porches and a wall with the neighboring unit, but the more expensive Colbert bungalows are totally detached and can comfortably sleep four. They cost $355 during the summer ($225 midweek in winter).

As its name suggests, the **Cottage Grove Inn** (1711 Lincoln Ave., Calistoga, 707/942-8400 or 800/799-2284, www.cottagegrove.com, $300-425) is actually 16 private cottages strung along a small road under a pretty grove of old elm trees on the edge of Calistoga. The cottages were built in 1996 and offer some modernity along a strip dominated by older motels. Despite their individual names, all 16 are furnished in a similar Mediterranean style with vaulted ceilings, beautiful antique wood floors, and a long list of luxury features including double Jacuzzi tub, CD and DVD player, fireplace, and front porch on which to sit, sip, and watch the world go by.

Calistoga was chosen to host the first resort created by Solage Hotels, a new brand from the exclusive Auberge Resorts chain that owns the staggeringly expensive Auberge du Soleil down in Rutherford. Opened in 2007, **Solage Calistoga** (755 Silverado Trail, Calistoga, 866/942-7442, www.solagecalistoga.com, $500) is best thought of as a baby Auberge, offering stylish contemporary accommodations for far less money. Being Calistoga, there's also a spa, but this one shares the resort's chic, modern style, although you'll pay extra to use it if you're not a hotel guest. Touted as the Napa Valley's first "affordable" resort, Solage is clearly targeted at a younger, more urban crowd than places like Auberge and Meadowood. Fashionable materials like polished concrete, pebbled floors in the steam showers, and plenty of dark wood complement the abundant technology in every room, from flat-screen TVs and CD players to wireless Internet access and iPod docks. A couple of cruiser bikes are parked outside each room; they're not touring quality, but they'll certainly get you into downtown Calistoga, a half mile away, and maybe to a few nearby wineries. Arriving here can be a little underwhelming because the trees planted on the grounds have yet to grow large enough to create a feeling of an oasis on what is otherwise a rather featureless patch of land bordering a trailer park, but once you're settled in this self-contained resort it's easy to forget the world outside. "Affordable" is a relative term for the resort, however. It's certainly affordable compared to Auberge du Soleil, but it's the top end of the scale for sleepy Calistoga. Some of the 83 studio-style rooms have fireplaces, minibars, and private patios. For more space at an extra $200, the six suites offer an extra sitting room.

Nearby is another member of the exclusive Auberge chain of resorts, this one hidden away on a wooded hillside with super-resort prices to match the glorious setting. The **Calistoga Ranch** (580 Lommel Rd., off Silverado Trail, Calistoga, 707/254-2800, www.calistogaranch.com, $900) is like a collection of exclusive lodges with a country-club atmosphere. Guests are relieved of their cars upon entering and whisked off up the hill to their rooms in golf carts. The accommodations consist of a series of rooms joined by a deck, with every conceivable luxury bell and whistle, from indoor-outdoor fireplaces and showers to plasma-screen TVs and wet bars. The smallest are 600 square feet, about double the average hotel room size and also double the average price around here. Expect to pay more for views of any kind, and for one of the apartment-sized one-bedroom lodges, approximately the amount many pay in monthly rent. For those who can bear to leave their luxury hideaways, there's the exclusive Bathhouse spa (treatments $75-260), outdoor pool, classes and seminars, and miles of hiking trails around the grounds.

FOOD

Calistoga is often overlooked in the valley's food scene, eclipsed by the culinary destinations of Yountville and St. Helena. High-end restaurants have struggled to survive here, as illustrated by the seemingly endless stream of restaurants that have tried, and failed, to make money in the town's fancy Mount View Hotel. Even the venerable Wappo Grill, a favorite of many valley residents and frequent visitors, could not survive the 2009 recession. And the FlatIron Grill shut its doors in 2012. But Calistoga continues to have good food at good prices, perhaps just a little more casual than its Napa Valley neighbors.

California Cuisine

Perhaps the hottest restaurant at the moment is the trendy **Solbar,** part of the luxurious Solage Calistoga resort (755 Silverado Trail, 707/226-0850, breakfast 7am-11:30am and lunch 11:45am-3pm daily, dinner 5:30pm-9pm Sun.-Thurs., 5:30pm-9:30pm Sat.-Sun., $30) at the eastern edge of town. The sleek

and contemporary indoor dining room is a fine backdrop for the innovative cuisine that gives farm fresh a modern twist. A confit of pork shoulder is paired with house-made pretzels, avocado parfait sits alongside ponzo-broiled hearts of palm, and a salad of endive and watercress is garnished with fennel pollen. The result is such that the restaurant has garnered a Michelin star every year from 2009 to 2013. But the biggest draw, at least in the summer and fall, is the spacious outdoor patio with its floating fireplace. With a couple of appetizers and a bottle of wine on a warm summer night, there's no better place for some up-valley people-watching and stargazing.

Walking past the 【 **Calistoga Inn** (1250 Lincoln Ave., Calistoga, 707/942-4101, www.calistogainn.com, lunch and dinner daily, dinner entrées $15-28) on a cool dark winter evening, it's tempting to go into the restaurant just for the cozy rustic atmosphere exuding through its Victorian windows. During the warmer months the draw is the creek-side patio, but nonetheless, all year the food is equally good bistro-style fare. Next door to the restaurant is an equally relaxed pub that's home to the **Napa Valley Brewing Company,** founded in 1989 and said to be the first brewery established in the valley since Prohibition. The inn also usually has some sort of evening entertainment, from open-mike nights to jazz.

A block down is **Brannan's Grill** (1374 Lincoln Ave., Calistoga, 707/942-2233, 3pm-9pm Mon.-Thurs., 11:30am-9:30pm Fri.-Sun., $20-35). White tablecloths, the 19th-century dark wood bar, and the giant murals of the valley's past lend an air of elegance to accompany the pricey all-American menu, which usually includes two or three steaks. The wine list offers a smattering of choices from Oregon, Europe, and Australia alongside Napa and Sonoma regulars. The emphasis is on the high-end, but offset by the $15 burger and side of mac and cheese. Try starting off the meal with a selection of Hog Island Oysters before you move on to their salads and bigger entrées. Desserts here are particularly good, especially the crème brûlée, if it happens to be on the menu that night.

The latest tenant to try to make a go of it in the Mount View Hotel is **JoLe** (1457 Lincoln Ave., Calistoga, 707/942-5938, www.jolerestaurant.com, 5pm-9pm Sun.-Thurs., 5pm-11pm Fri.-Sat., brunch 10am-2pm Sat.-Sun., $20), where the emphasis is on small plates of locally sourced, Mediterranean-inspired food in a contemporary setting. Select two or three dishes per person, such as sea scallops and sweetbreads with a parsnip puree or roasted quail with fingerling potatoes and Italian black cabbage, or try one of the tasting menus: You can pick from four, five, or six courses. The desserts (made by the second half of this husband and wife team) are just as sophisticated but a bit more playful, like the Campfire Cake made of house-made marshmallow and graham cracker. The list of local and international wines is well priced, and all but the most expensive wines are available by the glass and by the Pichet, which is about a half bottle. Like most up-and-coming restaurants, cocktails are a little more in the spotlight, focusing on fresh ingredients and artisanal spirits.

When trying to decide on a place to eat in Calistoga, don't be surprised if you find yourself lured in by leafy front patio of **Calistoga Kitchen** (1107 Cedar St., 707/942-6500, www.calistogakitchen.com, dinner 5:30pm-9pm Thurs.-Sat., lunch 11:30am-3pm Sat.-Sun., brunch 9:30am-3pm Sun., dinner entrées $25). And, as you peruse the menu, don't be surprised if owner and chef Rick Warkel approaches and tells you that your dogs, children, or anyone you have in tow are also welcome (an attitude not often found in the valley) and that his restaurant is one of the best in town— a boast you can find anywhere, but he may be right. The ingredients-driven menu, while slight, succeeds because everything on it is executed perfectly; you may never taste a more tender steak or a more delicate (and generously portioned) ahi. Even the salads, with toppings of duck and Cornish game hen, can stand alone as entrees. The wine selection is relatively short but carefully selected, with glasses available for

under $8. Lunch and brunch are a great bargain, and there is no better outdoor seating in all of Calistoga.

American

The roomy, exposed-brick interior of the **Hydro Bar & Grill** (1403 Lincoln Ave., Calistoga, 707/942-9777, dinner entrées $9-15) hints at its other life as a live-music venue, but it's also a place to get your standard American favorites at reasonable prices. Burgers, mac and cheese, salads, pork loin, and *steak frites* are some of the selections. But the bar is the draw. In addition to countless cocktail concoctions, there are plenty of microbrews, plus a full page (in small type) of wines, nearly all from the Napa Valley. It stays open well after most other restaurants have closed, which is good because the service can often be unbearably slow.

Barbecue

You'll know you've left behind the fussiness of St. Helena when you reach Calistoga's first intersection at Lincoln Avenue and see the Harleys lined up outside of **Buster's Barbecue and Bakery** (1207 Foothill Blvd., Calistoga, 707/942-5605, http://busterssouthernbbq.com, 10am-7pm Mon.-Sat., 10am-6pm Sun., $10). Opened in 1961, this walk-up eatery serves mostly locals looking for a quick bite to bring home. While the portions aren't huge, and prices are a bit high compared to other barbecue joints, the tri-tip sandwiches and barbecued chicken, pork, and ribs are often worth the trip. Expect traditional sides such as baked beans, slaw, potato salad, and corn bread to go with the vinegary and peppery sauce. The sweet-potato pie is a reputed local favorite, and for those eager to sit down with the food and a pile of napkins, there is a low-key dining area.

Italian

Sharing space with JoLe in the Mount View Hotel is the more casual **Barolo** (1457 Lincoln Ave., Calistoga, 707/942-9900, www.barolo-calistoga.com, dinner 4:30pm-9:30pm Sun.-Thurs., 4:30pm-10pm Fri.-Sat., $20). Its menu is traditional Italian trattoria with classic items like wood oven-fired margherita pizzas, Manilla clams cooked in white wine and garlic, house-made pastas, and entrées of chicken, pork, or short rib, while the interior is spare and modern decked out in black, red, and chrome. At the island bar you can nurse a cocktail with a name like "Sidewalks of Rome" or "Red Dragon" that is mixed, muddled, and shaken with the same finesse as at JoLe, or select a glass of wine from the wine menu that has equal selections of local and Italian wines. Both restaurants share the same chic "farm-to-table" ethos hip in today's Northern California dining scene.

Bosko's Trattoria (1364 Lincoln Ave., Calistoga, 707/942-9088, www.boskos.com, 11:30am-10pm daily, dinner entrées $17) is a Calistoga institution with a reputation for its Italian comfort food as solid as the stone building it calls home. The simple salads, some of the valley's best pastas, and wood-fired pizzas are served in the homey surroundings, as well as a good selection of delicious, well-stuffed panini sandwiches.

Mexican

Pacifico Mexican Restaurant (1237 Lincoln Ave., Calistoga, 707/942-4400, 11am-9pm Mon.-Thurs., 11am-10pm Fri., 10am-10pm Sat., 10am-9pm, $15) serves great south-of-the-border fare in a relaxed, easygoing atmosphere. When you first walk in, the restaurant feels cool, dark, and cavernous. There is a full bar, so be sure to order a margarita, if that is your fancy. If the weather is nice, take advantage of the outside seating along Cedar Street. Don't worry, you won't be forgotten (the staff is very friendly and attentive), and it is a great place to while away an afternoon or warm summer evening. The fajitas are especially good, as are the chiles rellenos; just be sure not to fill up on the chips and salsa that make it to your table upon arrival—the chips are warm, crisp, and fresh, while the house-made salsa is exceptional.

Breakfast and Brunch

For breakfast, try the old-fashioned **Café Sarafornia** (1413 Lincoln Ave., Calistoga, 707/942-0555, www.cafesarafornia.com,

7am-2:30pm daily, entrées $6-13), named for the famous verbal blunder by the town's founder, Sam Brannan. It is a favorite of locals, serving down-home, no-nonsense breakfast and brunch at the bar, booths, or tables. It also sells sandwiches to go ($8-10).

Delis

The ultracasual **Palisades Deli Café** (1458 Lincoln Ave., Calistoga, 707/942-0145, 7am-6pm daily, $8) occupies the bottom floor of the Depot's yellow station house. This counter-service deli has a huge selection of hot and cold sandwiches, burritos, tacos, salads, and wraps; all are flavorful, good sized, and tasty without feeling like a calorie bomb. The Ruben sandwich (known here as the Geyser) may rival any other made here in the valley. Espresso drinks are also available, as is a small but nice outside patio.

Picnic Supplies

Calistoga's mellow dining scene offers a number of places to grab picnic supplies and sandwiches to go. A great stop is the **Palisades Deli Café** (1458 Lincoln Ave., Calistoga, 707/942-0145, 7am-6pm daily). In addition to coffee and other café staples, it sells a range of deli meats and cheeses, chips, and cold drinks. You can also get any one of their freshly made sandwiches or wraps to go. If the line is too long, walk across the street to the **Cal Mart** supermarket (1491 Lincoln Ave., Calistoga, 707/942-4545, 7am-9pm daily), which sells even cheaper deli sandwiches (although not as good), a wide selection of cheese, and local wine.

Drop in to **Café Sarafornia** (1413 Lincoln Ave., Calistoga, 707/942-0555, www.cafesarafornia.com, 7am-2:30pm daily) to pick up one of its sandwiches, or for a gourmet alternative you could go to **Bosko's Trattoria** (1364 Lincoln Ave., Calistoga, 707/942-9088, www.boskos.com, 11:30am-10pm daily) and order a panini to go.

Farmers Market

The **Calistoga Farmers Market** (http://calistogafarmersmarket.org) is held 8:30am-noon on Saturday May-January at the Sharpsteen Museum Plaza at 1311 Washington Street. It sells crafts, cut flowers, oils and vinegars, crepes, and fresh seafood as well as produce.

INFORMATION AND SERVICES

The spacious **Calistoga Visitors Center** (1133 Washington St., Calistoga, 707/942-6333, www.calistogavisitors.org, 9am-5pm daily), located in the heart of downtown, has two walls where local wineries, restaurants, hotels, and spas leave brochures and discount passes for wineries, spa treatments, and restaurant meals. You'll even be able to grab the *Weekly Calistogan* for a dose of local news and up-and-coming events.

The **post office** is located at 1013 Washington Street. Nearby, the **Vermeil House Clinic** (913 Washington St., Calistoga, 707/942-6233, 9am-5pm Mon.-Fri.) is affiliated with the St. Helena Hospital and treats non-emergency health concerns. **Bank of the West** has a branch at 1317 Lincoln Avenue.

GETTING THERE AND AROUND

Calistoga is eight miles north of St. Helena on Highway 29. Highway 128 also runs through Calistoga, connecting it to U.S. Highway 101 north near Geyserville. From Santa Rosa, take exit 494 off U.S. Highway 101, labeled "River Rd/Guerneville." Turn right onto Mark West Springs Road and continue up the mountain. The road will miraculously change its name to Porter Creek Road in the process. Eventually, you'll come to a T intersection with Petrified Forest Road. Turn left and travel a few miles until you reach Highway 128. You can also connect to Porter Creek Road from the Highway 12 east exit. A left on Farmers Lane, then a right on Sonoma Highway will take you to Calistoga Road, onto which you turn left. After 7.1 miles, Calistoga Road intersects with Porter Creek Road.

You can also reach Calistoga by bus on the **VINE** (www.ridethevine.com, $1.50) on route 10, which makes daily runs up the valley from Napa. In Calistoga, you can catch the **Calistoga Shuttle** (707/963-4229), the VINE's on-demand shuttle service. All you have to do is call. The shuttle only goes within the city limits, and with a wait time of 15-20 minutes, it might be easier to have comfortable shoes and walk.

Another option is to rent a bike at the **Calistoga Bike Shop** (1318 Lincoln Ave., Calistoga, 707/942-9687 or 866/942-2453, www.calistogabikeshop.com, 10am-6pm daily). Hybrids run $35 per day, road bikes $45 per day, and mountain bikes $75 per day. For $80 you can opt for their self-guided Calistoga Cool Wine Tour, with which the bike shop will book your tastings, pay the fees, pick up any wine you buy, and provide any roadside assistance you may need.

www.moon.com

DESTINATIONS | ACTIVITIES | BLOGS | MAPS | BOOKS

MOON.COM is ready to help plan your next trip! Filled with fresh trip ideas and strategies, author interviews, informative travel blogs, a detailed map library, and descriptions of all the Moon guidebooks, Moon.com is all you need to get out and explore the world—or even places in your own backyard. While at Moon.com, sign up for our monthly e-newsletter for updates on new releases, travel tips, and expert advice from our on-the-go Moon authors. As always, when you travel with Moon, expect an experience that is uncommon and truly unique.

KEEP UP WITH MOON ON FACEBOOK AND TWITTER
JOIN THE MOON PHOTO GROUP ON FLICKR

MAP SYMBOLS

▦ Expressway	◖ Highlight	✗ Airfield	⚲ Golf Course
▬ Primary Road	○ City/Town	✗ Airport	◘ Parking Area
▬ Secondary Road	◉ State Capital	▲ Mountain	▰ Archaeological Site
▫ Unpaved Road	✪ National Capital	✚ Unique Natural Feature	⛪ Church
--- Trail	★ Point of Interest		
⋯ Ferry	• Accommodation	⟋ Waterfall	⛽ Gas Station
⋈ Railroad	▾ Restaurant/Bar	▲ Park	◌ Glacier
▨ Pedestrian Walkway	■ Other Location	⊓ Trailhead	▨ Mangrove
▥ Stairs	⋀ Campground	⛷ Skiing Area	▨ Reef
			▭ Swamp

CONVERSION TABLES

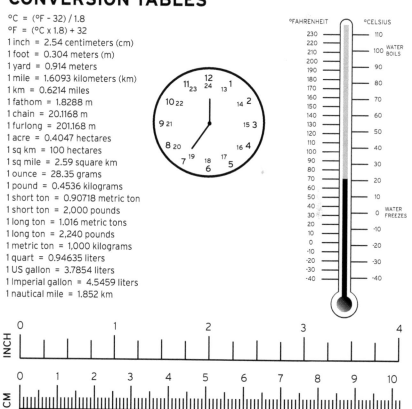

°C = (°F - 32) / 1.8
°F = (°C x 1.8) + 32
1 inch = 2.54 centimeters (cm)
1 foot = 0.304 meters (m)
1 yard = 0.914 meters
1 mile = 1.6093 kilometers (km)
1 km = 0.6214 miles
1 fathom = 1.8288 m
1 chain = 20.1168 m
1 furlong = 201.168 m
1 acre = 0.4047 hectares
1 sq km = 100 hectares
1 sq mile = 2.59 square km
1 ounce = 28.35 grams
1 pound = 0.4536 kilograms
1 short ton = 0.90718 metric ton
1 short ton = 2,000 pounds
1 long ton = 1.016 metric tons
1 long ton = 2,240 pounds
1 metric ton = 1,000 kilograms
1 quart = 0.94635 liters
1 US gallon = 3.7854 liters
1 Imperial gallon = 4.5459 liters
1 nautical mile = 1.852 km

MOON SPOTLIGHT NAPA VALLEY
Avalon Travel
a member of the Perseus Books Group
1700 Fourth Street
Berkeley, CA 94710, USA
www.moon.com

Editors: Erin Raber, Sabrina Young
Series Manager: Kathryn Ettinger
Copy Editor: Ann Seifert
Production and Graphics Coordinator: Darren Alessi
Cover Designer: Darren Alessi
Map Editor: Albert Angulo
Cartographers: Stephanie Poulain, Brian Shotwell,
 Kat Bennett

ISBN-13: 978-1-59880-677-9

Text © 2013 by Avalon Travel.
Maps © 2013 by Avalon Travel.
All rights reserved.

Some photos and illustrations are used by permission
 and are the property of the original copyright
 owners.

Front cover photo: Grapes on the vine, Fall, Napa
3510067 © Feverpitched | Dreamstime.com
Title page photo: © Chee-Onn Leong/123rf.com

Printed in the United States

Moon Spotlight and the Moon logo are the property
of Avalon Travel. All other marks and logos depicted
are the property of the original owners. All rights
reserved. No part of this book may be translated or
reproduced in any form, except brief extracts by a
reviewer for the purpose of a review, without written
permission of the copyright owner.

All recommendations, including those for sights,
activities, hotels, restaurants, and shops, are based
on each author's individual judgment. We do not
accept payment for inclusion in our travel guides,
and our authors don't accept free goods or services
in exchange for positive coverage.

Although every effort was made to ensure that
the information was correct at the time of going
to press, the author and publisher do not assume
and hereby disclaim any liability to any party for any
loss or damage caused by errors, omissions, or any
potential travel disruption due to labor or financial
difficulty, whether such errors or omissions result
from negligence, accident, or any other cause.

KEEPING CURRENT

If you have a favorite gem you'd like to see included in the next edition, or see anything
that needs updating, clarification, or correction, please drop us a line. Send your com-
ments via email to feedback@moon.com, or use the address above.

ABOUT THE AUTHOR

© GERRIT VENEMAN

Elizabeth Linhart Veneman

Elizabeth Linhart Veneman has always viewed growing up in Northern California as both a blessing and curse. There is so much to see, do, and experience all within a short drive — from broad sequoias in the Sierra to ancient lava beds north of Mount Shasta, from creaky Gold Rush towns to the pampering Wine Country — that she began to wonder why anyone would ever leave.

Elizabeth was eventually lured out of the Golden State to Alaska's far north, where she traveled the Inside Passage, baked bread under the midnight sun in Denali National Park, and chronicled the state's burgeoning sustainable agriculture for *Alaska Magazine*. These adventures culminated in penning *InsightGuides: Alaska*.

But Elizabeth knew her California roots were too deep to stay away for long. Raised in Carmel, where her great-great grandmother opened the town's first restaurant (a soup kitchen with dirt floors!) at the turn of the 20th century, she will always call California home. So she returned and devoted herself to writing about the state she loves most. Her work has included *SmartGuide: San Francisco* and *InsightGuides: San Francisco*. She also reports on food and sustainable agriculture for local publications.

Elizabeth currently lives with her family in San Francisco.

WITHDRAWN

31901055347282